GROWING UP IN
LA COLONIA

GROWING UP IN

LA COLONIA

Boomer Memories from Oxnard's Barrio

MARGO PORRAS & SANDRA PORRAS

THE
History
PRESS

Published by The History Press
Charleston, SC
www.historypress.com

Front cover, top: *Left to right*: Irene Vera, Ofelia Espinoza and Eugenio Lujan in Ramona School, La Colonia, Oxnard, 1958. *Courtesy of Lupe Lujan*; *bottom*: Agricultural fields, Oxnard, 2018. *Photo by the author*.
Back cover, top left: Lemon harvest, Oxnard, 1940s. *Courtesy of Bungalow Productions*; *top right*: Muñoz and Ortiz families, La Colonia, Oxnard, early 1940s. *Courtesy of Martha Muñoz Rodriguez*; *bottom*: Velas placed before the statue of the Virgen de Guadalupe at Our Lady of Guadalupe Church, La Colonia, Oxnard, December 2018. *Photo by the author*.

First published 2019

Manufactured in the United States

ISBN 9781467141819

Library of Congress Control Number: 2019936986

CONTENTS

Preface   7
Acknowledgements   11
Introduction. "Or the Colonia"   13

1. The Way It Was in La Colonia: "It Was Our Whole World"   23
2. Home, Food and Family: "There Was No One Else Like Us"   34
3. Called to Serve: La Colonia Joins the Ranks   53
4. Work: *La Pisca*, but So Much More   61
5. Unrest, Activism and Progress: "Aggressive in Spirit"   79
6. Roberto: "Due in La Colonia"   102
7. The Churches   109
8. School Days   124

Epilogue. *Chiques*   147
Bibliography   149
Recommended Reading for All Ages   155
About the Authors   157

PREFACE

alk through the barrio of La Colonia on a Sunday morning and you'll likely hear a rooster crowing, a distant train, the sound of hard-soled "dressy" shoes crunching on pavement and laughter. Laughter of children spending their energy before having to sit still in a pew. Laughter of *comadres* as they tease each other over a bit of *chisme*. Laughter of neighbors as they finally have a moment to catch up on their misadventures of the past week. People from the Colonia love to laugh, though the things they laugh about are real. Morning sounds in La Colonia take on an otherworldly, insulated quality, muffled and sharpened at the same time by the ever-present fog. To an outsider, it can be downright startling. But then of course, if you're walking through the Colonia on a Sunday morning, it's almost certainly because you're from the barrio yourself.

The city of Oxnard is an often-overlooked spot on California's historic southern coast. It is sometimes considered a backwater, lacking the bright showbiz lights of Los Angeles or the romance of Santa Barbara, its closest neighbors. Its nickname, the "Gateway to the Channel Islands," hardly describes what or who one might find there. But if Oxnard can be said to be known for anything at all, it's for agriculture in general and strawberries in particular.

The Strawberry Festival has been the highlight of the Oxnard calendar for over thirty-five years. It annually draws up to sixty thousand attendees, many of whom arrive by car, driving through miles of strawberry fields to celebrate the storied fruit. Some decide to make a weekend of it, staying to take in the

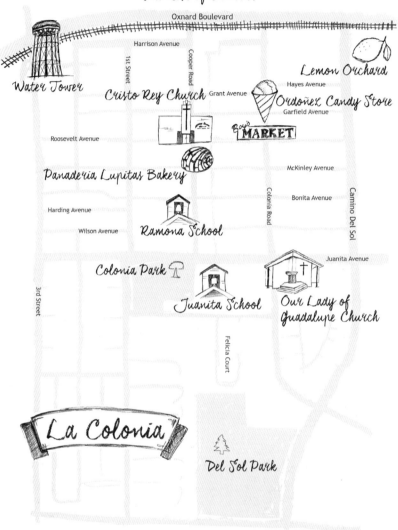

The Rest of Oxnard↑

Oxnard Boulevard

Harrison Avenue

1st Street

Cooper Road

Grant Avenue

Hayes Avenue

Garfield Avenue

Roosevelt Avenue

Water Tower

Cristo Rey Church

Lemon Orchard

Ordoñez Candy Store

Boy's MARKET

Panadería Lupitas Bakery

McKinley Avenue

Colonia Road

Bonita Avenue

Camino Del Sol

Harding Avenue

Wilson Avenue

Ramona School

3rd Street

Colonia Park

Juanita Avenue

Juanita School

Our Lady of Guadalupe Church

Felicia Court

La Colonia

Del Sol Park

Map of La Colonia by Joey Hendrix. *Courtesy of the artist.*

8

beautiful beaches and tour some of Oxnard's historic sights. They'll learn about the rich farming history of the area—not just strawberries but beans, lemons and the crop that started it all, the one that gave Oxnard its name: the sugar beet. Such visitors generally receive little to no information about the masses of laborers behind this history.

It takes a lot of people to run an agricultural empire. If few have ever heard of Oxnard, even fewer have heard of the barrio that keeps it running. For generations, the majority of those who work the fields surrounding Oxnard have been Latinos. Though sometimes obscured by the official public story of the city, Latinos nevertheless make up about 75 percent of its current population, many with roots in, or ties to, the barrio of *La Colonia*, which translated means "The Colony."

The story of La Colonia is colorful, if virtually invisible to visitors. Its citizens, past and present, lovingly recall their time there in spite of the trials they constantly endured. Against the backdrop of their day-to-day *lucha*, a rich microculture evolved. One that has produced affordable food for the entire country, to be sure, but has also produced landmark movements in labor and education, prizefighters, artists, military heroes and brushes with history, such as the "Pachuco riots" or the time Bobby Kennedy stopped to pray in the barrio's little cinderblock church of Cristo Rey just eight days before he was assassinated.

Oxnard High School Marching Band performs at Strawberry Festival, Oxnard, 2018. *Photo by author.*

Agricultural fields, Oxnard, 2018. *Photo by author.*

The fact is, every strawberry you've ever tasted has been picked by someone taking part in a very compelling story. It's a story that began before California became part of the United States and continues to flavor the lives and families of every person who has ever lived in La Colonia.

ACKNOWLEDGEMENTS

This is a collective memoir, spanning several decades and capturing as many people's stories as we could in the time allowed. It's been a profound privilege to join their firsthand accounts about this special place with historical signposts to put them in context.

Our purpose with this project was to share the feelings of warmth and closeness experienced by families like ours, even years after leaving the Colonia. The many families quoted in this book were extraordinarily generous. They allowed us into their homes and gave us access to their archives of photos and treasured heirlooms. We thank them all from the bottom of our hearts for allowing us to share their important stories.

There were also participants who were not necessarily from the Colonia but who nevertheless went out of their way to share their time and knowledge with us. We'd like to thank the librarians and assistants at Oxnard Public Library, the Museum of Ventura County and the Los Angeles Public Library, as well as Sylvia Mendez and the Mendez family for allowing us to share their historic photo. We also thank Laurie Krill and the entire team at The History Press for their support.

Additionally, we'd like to express our gratitude to the academics who contributed to this book, either personally or through their groundbreaking work, including Dr. David G. Garcia and Dr. Frank Barajas for their painstakingly researched books about Oxnard, *Strategies of Segregation* and *Curious Unions*, respectively. It was Dr. Barajas who first shared with us the "Colonia" series by Don W. Martin that is mentioned throughout this book.

ACKNOWLEDGEMENTS

Dr. Isidro Ortiz graciously allowed us to use an excerpt from a lecture he gave at the San Diego Public Library in the fall of 2018 and connected us with Dr. Elvia Estrella. Dr. Richard Griswold del Castillo gave us valuable historical background in an interview conducted near Christmas 2018.

Lupe Lopez Lujan was critically important in helping us with virtually every aspect of our research, including making enormous pots of *caldo* to keep us going. She introduced us to many people who brought diversity and a wealth of knowledge to the project. We truly could not have written this without her help.

I would also personally like to thank my mother, Sandra Porras, for her help with interviews, transcribing, driving and mostly for her support. Her own experiences, though never quoted, were present in the memories of everyone included in this book.

We humbly dedicate this entire project, *con amor, a la gente de La Colonia*—especially the kids from Hayes Street, near the lemon orchard.

—Margo Porras

"OR THE COLONIA"

What is Colonia? Virtually everyone in Oxnard must know where it is, but only those who live there know just what *it is.*
—*Don W. Martin,* Oxnard Press-Courier, *July 1963*

In July 1963, journalist Don W. Martin wrote a five-part series on the neighborhood of La Colonia for the *Oxnard Press-Courier*. It covered the barrio from several angles: housing issues, discrimination faced by Colonia residents, the role of the church in the community and a day in the life of a typical Colonia laborer. The series was written in response to the cancellation of an urban renewal plan that could have brought about greatly improved quality of life for Colonia residents. Martin referred to the area as "Oxnard's Stepchild" because of its strange relationship to the small town in which it is nestled.

Many readers of the *Press-Courier* in 1963 would have never seen La Colonia, even though it is literally steps away from downtown Oxnard. In the first article of his series, Martin addresses the questions residents of Greater Oxnard typically had about the barrio, asking, "Is Colonia a ghetto for minority groups? Or a humane refuge for low income families that can't afford higher rents? Do people live there by choice, or by force through sociological or economic pressure?"

Martin's questions are remarkably relevant today. To answer them, it's necessary to trace the history of the region from its earliest origins.

The caption on this photo, from Don Martin's Colonia series, reads "This Is Colonia," 1963. *Image from* Oxnard Press-Courier.

The caption on this photo, from Don Martin's Colonia series, reads "So Is This," 1963. *Image from* Oxnard Press-Courier.

The area now known as Oxnard, California, originally belonged to the indigenous Chumash, who have lived in the area for over thirteen thousand years. Chumash cave paintings dating back over one thousand years can be seen at Chumash Painted Cave State Historic Park in nearby Santa Barbara, depicting a society that thrived in the fertile landscape. There are currently two to five thousand Chumash still living in California, but when the Spanish first arrived, in the late eighteenth century, they numbered an estimated fifteen thousand. The Spanish and Mexican era in California history lasted roughly from the 1760s to the 1840s; it was rocky at best for the indigenous culture on whom it was imposed.

Near the end of the Spanish and Mexican period, in 1834, the land on which Oxnard now sits was granted to some former soldiers of the Santa Barbara Presidio; grant holders of this type are usually referred to as "Californios." The grant was called "Rancho El Rio de Santa Clara o la Colonia," which translated means "Ranch of the River of Saint Clare or the Colony."

It was a strange period in California's history. Dr. Richard Griswold del Castillo, professor emeritus of Chicano studies at San Diego State University, sheds some light on this turbulent time:

> *The Californios, in general, were not farmers. They were ranchers, they had cattle and sheep; that was their main industry in Southern and Northern California. So the Indians worked as vaqueros (cowboys), as well as doing what farming was necessary to raise grains and crops like that. In fact, it was devalued as an occupation to be a farmer in those days because it was the working class, the Indians, that farmed. Then, in California, the Americans came in and they found these expanses of land, and there was no farming on it, just cattle. So they squatted. They took it over and built their houses there.*
>
> *The squatters got together and demanded that the federal government do something about the titles and the land situation in California because they were coming in all the time and finding out that the land was claimed by other people. So they pushed the senator from California [William M. Gwin, in 1851] to introduce a law to the Congress that would require that all land grant holders in California would have to prove their ownership before a commission within two years. If they failed to do so, then the land would be considered part of the public domain, which meant anybody could settle on it.*
>
> *So what that did was to throw up in the air the land titles of the Californios. The problem was that many of the land grant holders had not completed the process for legitimizing their land grants under the Mexican*

government. So they didn't have all the paperwork in order, and when they went to the land commission, they had to fight that situation.

    But it turned out that the railroads and mining companies…and large speculators wanted to get that land, so they dragged it out in court. They got lawyers and they fought against the Californios in court.

Litigation over the Gwin Land Act, sometimes called the California Land Act of 1851, created an impossible situation for many Mexican landholders. A few such cases were litigated all the way into the 1940s. Dr. Griswold del Castillo clarifies:

Eventually, the costs of that [litigation], *plus the fact it sometimes took up to thirty years for a land grant holder to get approved after filing by the court, meant that most of the landowners lost their lands to the lawyers and banks. They had to mortgage it to pay the taxes, the lawyers, etc. It's a tragic situation, but that's the larger picture and probably was what happened to the grants in the Ventura area as well. If they needed the money to pay the land taxes, which had gone up, they would be forced to sell.*

So even when land grants were ultimately declared valid, as in the case of the Rancho El Rio de Santa Clara o la Colonia grant, owners often found themselves in a precarious position. But the land act wasn't the only obstacle Mexican landholders faced.

There was also a law passed that required that everyone put up a fence around their land, a fence law. So that was a very expensive proposition, too, if you have 300,000 or 400,000 acres of property to put a fence around. So [the Californios] *needed money for that, they'd go to the bank and try to borrow money…and then the cattle prices started falling around the 1870s. The cattle industry was going down. They had a drought and a flood* [that] *wiped out a lot of the cattle, in terms of numbers, but there were also competitive sources coming from overland, other sources of food coming in besides the cattle. With the price of cattle going down, they didn't have enough money to pay for all of the expenses that were involved, so they had to sell for whatever they could get.*

    The legal system was against the Mexican landholders. There were lots of shady deals and pressures and even violence, especially up north, directed against the Mexicans. They couldn't get justice in the courts. So that was a hard lesson—that, even though they were citizens and landholders, they were being pressured to give it up because of the American aggression, of Manifest Destiny and so forth.

Eventually, Rancho El Rio de Santa Clara o la Colonia was purchased from the last of its Californio owners, and its main industry evolved from cattle to agriculture.

SUGAR, SUGAR: OXNARD BECOMES A BOOMTOWN

In 1966, Don Martin, the same journalist who had written the Colonia series in the *Press-Courier* three years earlier, recounted a popular yarn about how the city of Oxnard got its name.

Henry Thomas Oxnard Built a Factory, and Created a Town from a Barley Field

There was more static than conversation in that long distance telephone conversation from Sacramento to the new Pacific Beet Sugar Company factory in Ventura County in 1898. But then, the telephone had barely emerged from the experimental stage in those days.

"Sir, the senate is about to act on the name you proposed for this new town," said the voice from Sacramento. "But nobody here knows how to pronounce it."

"It's 'Sakchar.' You pronounce it 'Sak-kar,' with the accent on the last syllable." Henry T. Oxnard shouted into the receiver, "I'm calling the town that because it's the Greek word for sugar. And we're building one of the world's largest sugar refineries here."

"What?" said the voice from Sacramento, which, incidentally belonged to the secretary of the senate.

"Sak-kar! SAK-KAR!" Henry bellowed.

"Sakwhat?"

"Oh, hell!" Henry snapped into the uncooperative telephone, "Just call it Oxnard!"

And this, according to Mrs James G. Oxnard of Albuquerque, a niece of Henry T. Oxnard, is how the City of Oxnard got its name.

Incidentally, *sakchar*, with the accent on the last syllable, is not the Greek word for sugar. The pronunciation as described in the story is, however, very close to the *Turkish* word for sugar, *şeker*. It's a cute story, but it makes a point. Oxnard owes its very existence to the beet sugar business.

Above: American Beet Sugar Factory built by Henry T. Oxnard, 1930s. *Image from* Oxnard Press-Courier.

Left: Women among sacks of sugar in the American Beet Sugar Factory, 1940s. *Image from* Oxnard Press-Courier.

The booming agricultural industry of Oxnard in the early twentieth century quickly spread far beyond sugar beets. As many an Oxnard resident will tell you, "You can grow anything here!" But agriculture needs manpower, and the demographics of Oxnard's labor force changed dramatically throughout the early 1900s. According to Dr. Griswold del Castillo, there were surprisingly few Mexicans left in the area at that time:

By the time the agricultural industry takes hold, a lot of the Mexicans had been displaced from their land, when the ranchos were sold. They used to be able to live on the ranchos without paying anything. And then somebody buys it and says, "Okay, well you've got to pay me rent." So that would be an incentive to move on to another place, for a job and so forth. The cattle industry was not a place where they could earn a living anymore. So they had to go somewhere else to earn a living.

So, typically, [agriculture in the late nineteenth century] *wanted a labor force that they could control easily, that they could deport easily, pay low wages, etc. Mexicans were there during that period, but there weren't that many—yet. The preference of the big industrial farmers at that time was for Asian workers, to start with. In Oxnard, one of the first agricultural strikes was by the Japanese workers, around 1903.* [After that,] *they didn't want Japanese workers anymore because they were causing too much trouble in terms of organizing.*

Gradually, though, the agriculture industry brought in more and more laborers of Mexican descent throughout the early twentieth century. The area now known as La Colonia became more defined as the American Beet Sugar Company (ABSC) built adobe housing for workers, many of whom had come from Mexico fleeing the revolution. Fred Rodriguez, whose family arrived in Oxnard during that period, recalls the housing conditions his family had access to when they first arrived in La Colonia:

My father came in 1917 with two brothers; they'd been a family of at least ten. All the other brothers had gotten killed during the Mexican revolution, along with one sister. The interesting thing was, they were all on different sides. Their father got the [remaining] *three sons together and said, "We're leaving this country." That's how they came in 1917. Our houses here were made from two old horse stables, one for my* tío *and one for my father. They were redwood slats.*

Betabeleros of La Colonia, the workers who harvested the sugar beets, pose with their machetes, 1930s. *Courtesy of Bungalow Productions.*

Mexican passport of the Muñoz family, one of many who fled the revolution and found their way Oxnard, August 29, 1918. *Courtesy of Martha Muñoz Rodriguez.*

In his book *Curious Unions*, Dr. Frank Barajas offers more insight on the establishment of La Colonia as a district designed to house farm and factory labor:

> *A large number of* betabeleros [laborers in the beet fields] *and their families…lived in the adobe homes built and owned by the ABSC. The Mexican community over time concentrated in the district of La Colonia… along with blacks and various ethnic Asian residents, mainly Japanese and Filipinos. The dominant white population lived principally west of Oxnard Boulevard. With the early segregated development of Oxnard's residential spaces emerged corollary institutions of education and religion, particularly the Catholic Church.*
>
> *…The Southern Pacific spur railroad line—and the subsequent construction of ice, packing and food-processing plants after World War II—buffered the town from the emergent Mexican barrio enclave that literally placed La Colonia residents on the other side of the tracks.*

Sequestered from the rest of Oxnard, La Colonia evolved on its own over time. Its residents had, by necessity, to learn to adapt and utilize the resources they had available to them. It was not an easy existence. Throughout the barrio's history, *la gente* would face many challenges, but they would also create treasured memories and forge lifelong bonds.

CHAPTER 1

THE WAY IT WAS IN LA COLONIA

"It Was Our Whole World"

What I remember about the Colonia is that it was our whole world. We literally lived on the other side of the tracks. We were not isolated, but we were insulated, like an island that has a boat to cross to the other side.

It was the center of everybody's life. Everything was there. Everybody knew everybody. It was a complete life. I did not realize what I was missing, what was lacking. On TV you noticed people had other things, but our life was complete. On our block alone there were nine of us kids in our house, a family next door with ten, another across the street with fifteen. Our world, the kids' world, was the street. We made up games, played in the dirt, made our own stilts. We created our own world. We had everything we needed.

That's how Colonia native Ofelia Rodriguez remembers the barrio where she and her eight siblings were born, on the little block of North Hayes Avenue (usually referred to as Hayes Street), near the lemon orchard in Oxnard, in the late 1940s.

A decade earlier, *another* family arrived in La Colonia. They moved onto the block behind Ofelia's home. A series of misfortunes had cost them the home they'd always known in Arizona, and like many American families of Mexican descent, they'd come west as the Great Depression ended.

Librado, the father, had come out to Oxnard first. Once he found work, he sent for his wife, Juana, and their remaining children: Richard, Cesar, Rita and Vicky. The family had already lost a daughter, Helena, before leaving Arizona. After arriving in La Colonia, they endured many more hardships. The couple's younger son, Cesar Chavez, would remember his

House on Garfield Street, La Colonia, 2018. The Chavez family lived behind this house in a storage shed in the late 1930s. *Photo by author.*

first winter in Oxnard as the worst of his life. In *Cesar Chavez: Autobiography of La Causa*, Chavez shared his first impressions:

> *Oxnard is a damp, foggy little town near the Pacific ocean about fifty-five miles north of Los Angeles.…Winter in Oxnard is wet and cold. When it isn't raining, the fog pours in thick from the Pacific, leaving drops of water on everything it touches.*
>
> *…Though farm workers were harvesting vegetables and fruit, hunger was constant.…Some families survived on nothing but beans and fried dough, or perhaps just fried oatmeal, or dandelion greens and boiled potatoes.*
>
> *…When we found the little house in the barrio, we piled out of the car to explore our new surroundings. A weathered fence around the yard turned that shack into a fort. That's the way it was in La Colonia— many houses in one lot, very small houses, and lots of people in each house, unpaved streets, no lights, no sewers, just outhouses. And every house had a fence.*

Above: Oxnard neighborhood, 2018. The roads, sidewalks and unfenced yards are much as they were by the 1920s. *Photo by author.*

Left: McKinley Street, La Colonia, 1947. Unpaved roads with new sidewalks, background. Before then, every house needed to have a fence for safety. *Courtesy of Bungalow Productions.*

For most of the twentieth century, La Colonia was, in many ways, decades behind the rest of Oxnard. By the 1920s, the other side of the tracks had broad paved roads, sidewalks and homes with electricity and indoor plumbing—amenities not extended to the barrio.

IT WAS A WONDERFUL LIFE

Manuel Muñoz, who was born in La Colonia in 1939, recalls life in the barrio in the years during and after World War II:

Pearl Harbor was bombed in '41. The whole western United States was afraid that the Japanese would bomb the West Coast. All the villages on the coast were on alert. During the war, my father was an air raid warden; they had blackouts. We had kerosene lamps, and we had to put a black curtain on our windows. No sidewalks, no paved streets, no asphalt. We had boardwalks. I remember running around with shoes that had holes in the bottom for a long time.

We would go around and make sure everybody in the Colonia had their curtains closed, that there were no lights getting out. We had a big old siren to alert everybody. We'd practice getting under the table and so on, in case a bombing occurred. I used to walk with my dad. I was a tiny guy.

It was dangerous; you know why? We were surrounded! We had Port Hueneme naval base and we had Point Mugu, and so on. We were a target.

It was hard times getting back up on our feet after the war. We had to ration stamps; a loaf of bread would cost twenty-five cents. Milk cost ten cents a bottle. We survived, but it was interesting because it was the only way you learned about life itself, during a crisis like that.

You know where Rose and Colonia Road meet? There used to be, way back then, a big pipe that let out a bunch of water from farming areas. We used to call it our old swimming hole. It's where you'd go to get cool when it got hot. The water pipe is still there. There was a eucalyptus tree right next to it. We used to tie a rope around one of the branches and hang on old tires and jump in.

We'd play hide-and-go-seek underneath the houses. There were spiders all over the place! And we'd chop wood for our wood-burning stoves.

Absolutely, we had an outhouse! We had one until 1950, more or less. We used to have a lot of bedpans, too. With ten of us in the house, it was a lot. Can you imagine that? So, if you wanted to go to

Neighbors among Colonia wildflowers, Oxnard, 1940s. *Courtesy of Martha Muñoz Rodriguez.*

La Colonia Boxing Gym, now located within the old firehouse, has turned out some formidable figures in the sport's history. *Photo by author.*

the bathroom at night, you had to get the lantern, light it up and then go outside and go for it.

We collected blue chip and green chip stamps, and we'd turn them in for some prize. All we had was radio; we didn't have TV yet. I loved the westerns like Roy Rogers, Gene Autry, Tom Mix. We used to have county fair parades, and celebrities from the world of westerns used to come. We were happy; I was anyway. I loved everything.

It was quite interesting, actually. There was a togetherness of life. We helped each other out: "What do you need? Okay, come with me."

IT SMELLED SO BEAUTIFUL

Robert "Bob" Herrera, who owned Bob's Market, also remembers the barrio during the war years:

We didn't know what segregation was. That's how our mentalities were. I just love everybody, I don't distinguish. When others do, I say, "No, we are all children of God." It's not right [to discriminate], *you know?*

I remember las lámparas de queroseno, cuando levantaron, así [the gas lamps they'd light when they got up in the morning, like that]. *We didn't miss it, not having electricity. We'd go to bed early anyway.*

In our family's case, we didn't play in the street. Our Aunt Jessie was very strict. She used to keep us in the yard, but it was wonderful. She would take us to the five-and-ten-cent store, the Woolworth's here in Oxnard, on Saturdays or Sundays. She'd buy us the orange slices, loose candy, which I liked. She got us hooked on those. She was a wonderful lady.

When there were no sidewalks or streets en La Colonia, it was clean. I remember my grandma, my mom, everybody would get up in the morning and sweep the street, sweep the dirt. But it's a blessing, you know why? Because they put water to keep the dust down, and the dirt smelled so beautiful. See? It's God's creation.

IT WAS A LOT OF FUN

Ofelia Cabral was born on First Street in La Colonia just before World War II. She recalls many fun times with the neighborhood kids during the 1950s:

We played out in the street with all of our friends. The Colonia was a nice neighborhood. All the parents had a lot of kids, so we had a lot of people to play with. At night in the summertime we would all go outside and play tag. We had a lot of fun when we were young.

When we started growing up, we would go out to parties. We used to go in bunches, not one-and-one; all the girls would go and all the boys would go. It was a lot of fun in the old days. Out on Cooper Road, the cars would drive up and down, and the girls would walk along the streets and the boys would pick up the girls. We would go down to the park then back up Cooper and down to Hayes. It was the same route all the time. That was a Saturday night hangout. That's what they would do.

The parties, we would go to people's homes as they would do in those days. They didn't really drink. They used to dance, and we used to talk with each other. All the girls would hang out together. It was a lot of fun.

Colonia house party, Oxnard, late 1950s. *Courtesy of Martha Muñoz Rodriguez.*

LITTLE BY LITTLE, WE WERE ABSORBING BITS OF CULTURE

As the 1960s unfolded, homes in the barrio began to have access to TV and rock-and-roll music. As Louis Estrada recalls, life for the Colonia kids was slowly changing:

Even though I lived in the Colonia, I never had the awareness of how different my life was from what I was seeing on TV. I remember Sky King *and* The Rifleman…*everyone watched them. Little by little, we were absorbing bits of culture we weren't seeing around the neighborhood. We didn't stop to think about whether or not it was Mexicano.*

It was like in the Charlie Brown comics, where the kids all communicate only with each other and when the adults speak, it's like "woh-woh-woh." The parents let us just play and didn't insert themselves too much; they didn't get involved in what we were doing.

Everyone would meet in the alley by our house because we were in the middle of the block. It was great because it was easy for me to run inside while we were playing and grab something to eat. My grandma would get after me, "Get back outside!" There was never a reason to go into anyone's house. We were a group of kids that were a unit, and the parents weren't part of that.

Eugenio Lujan, *right*, and cousin, Oxnard, late 1950s. *Courtesy of Lupe Lopez Lujan.*

Wilson Junior High School graduation, Oxnard, 1960s. *Courtesy of Martha Muñoz Rodriguez.*

> *When we played, we would use the whole neighborhood, all the blocks and the alleys running between them, vacant lots. They seemed so vast, but now when I go back, they are so minute! I'm amazed how, as an adult, it seems like the neighborhood shrunk somehow.*
>
> *When we were little, it wasn't easy for my grandmother to get us ready for school. Because our home was built before the 1930s and it was so dilapidated, the toilet was outside of the house, there was an outhouse. We went there.*
>
> *We didn't have any means of taking baths other than our grandmother bringing out the* tina [basin used for laundry]. *She'd do three of them! She would prepare the water, and we would take baths outside. We only took baths once a week. On days that we had to go to school, she would get a washcloth and clean our arms, our necks, our faces.*

Colonia native Rachel Martinez Sandoval remembers the family atmosphere that pervaded the Colonia: "We could give you a list of all the families we knew when we lived there…but it would be a big list."

WHEN ARE WE GOING TO GO SEE GRANDMA?

In the 1970s, many baby boomers had moved out of the Colonia, but they maintained close ties with their relatives and friends who still lived in the barrio. Dr. Elvia Estrella recalls adjusting to her family's move to Oxnard's West Side in the 1970s:

I'd always ask my mom why we moved. "Why are we here, Mom? We eat chicharrones." *She'd say,* "Cállate, pendeja, *we have a nice house, and this is a nice neighborhood." I think maybe she was trying to convince herself in the process. When my mom and dad were growing up, everybody lived in La Colonia. Then they moved out to try to become more successful. So you got out, but you always went back.*

For a long time, I would always be asking, "When are we going to go see Grandma?" Because when we went to the Colonia, we would get to play in the street. We could play there! It was safe. It was comfortable. I just remember that sense of...everybody knew everybody. "O sí, la mamá de Pancho..."

The cultural composition in Colonia was all Latinos and African Americans; everybody played together. My cousins Gloria and Sylvia were older, but they were the only other ones who spoke English. I loved going there and hanging out with them because they understood me.

Children celebrating Cinco de Mayo at Ramona School, La Colonia, Oxnard, early 1980s. *Courtesy of Martha Muñoz Rodriguez.*

Offerings for the Day of Our Lady of Guadalupe, Colonia, 2018. *Photo by author.*

In many ways, Dr. Estrella's family brought the Colonia with them when they moved to the West Side:

Even though we lived on the West Side, we went to 6:30 a.m. Mass in the Colonia for many, many years—even though our home parish was really St. Anthony's and the diocese made us do our sacraments there. Mom would take us to Mass every Sunday at Our Lady of Guadalupe. Sometimes I was bad; I would sneak out and come back whenever I wanted. But my mom knew. So she would come and wake me up at five o'clock the next morning:

"Knock, knock! Are you ready? Get up. We're going to Our Lady of Guadalupe."

"But Mom…"

So there we'd be, in the first pew with whatever priest it was in the cycle; we got them all. My grandfather is ninety-four now, and until a couple of years ago he'd wake up every morning and go to church there at Our Lady of Guadalupe. I really admire that.

Whenever I think of the Colonia, it makes me smile and laugh.

CHAPTER 2

HOME, FOOD AND FAMILY

"There Was No One Else Like Us"

After we moved to the West Side [of Oxnard], *my dad would grow corn in the front yard. Every year we would have to take the corn off the husk. My dad took most of our backyard for corn, too. I'd be like, "Are you kidding me? Dad, we are not doing this. We are* not *doing this!" That was when I started getting older. I'd swear I was in Indiana or something.*

Everybody in the Colonia had to have a chile *plant and* guayabas. *We had a pomegranate plant, sweet and sour. We had* aguacate, calabasas, tomates, cebollas, el elote [avocado, squash, tomato, onion, corn]. *Oh wait,* nopales [prickly pear cactus] *were a staple. My grandma still has the* nopales *there at her house in the Colonia. And we haven't even hit the herbs!* Yerba buena, romero, *cilantro, oregano…*

I'd always be like, "Qué? Que te tengo que agarrar?" [What? What do you want me to get for you?]

"Traeme una rama de romero!" [Bring me a sprig of rosemary!]
"Cual es romero, Mamí?" [Which one's rosemary, Mom?]
"El que está allá!" [The one over there!]
"Pues, yo no sé…" [Um, I don't know though…]
"Ándale y apúrate, agarralo!" [Hurry up and get it already!]

I didn't know what on earth this herb or that herb was; I'd just come back with bunches and she'd be like, "You brought me the wrong one!"

My mom still has the corner of her house with the little bricks, with nopales, oregano, cilantro. *The* romero, *I learned, was in the front. It was a bad omen if you didn't have a* romero *plant. "Why do you have that? That smells gross, Mom."*
"Cause you have to."
—Dr. Elvia Estrella

Family gathering, La Colonia, Oxnard, late 1950s. *Courtesy of Lupe Lopez Lujan.*

REVIVING THE TRADITION

Today, many of the old front yard gardens of La Colonia, in which corn and *tomates* once flourished, are long gone. Now that there are more people living in the old houses and—unlike in the old days—everyone has their own car, many front yards have been paved over to compensate for the lack of parking space on the neighborhood's narrow streets. Throughout the 1980s and 1990s, many residents of the barrio no longer had even the little bit of earth they once had to grow some of their own fresh food. La Colonia was in danger of becoming another one of America's "food deserts," a residential area with little to no access to fresh produce.

But a few years ago, the City of Oxnard opened a community garden at the end of Hayes and Garfield Streets, where the old lemon orchard once stood. Eric Humel, who oversees the garden, describes how it has been incorporated into La Colonia, reviving for many the tradition of growing vegetables, fruits and herbs:

> *I'd say it's at least 50 percent people from the Colonia. There's a lot of people who garden there who are from the north side of Camino Del Sol.*

Corn growing in community garden, La Colonia, Oxnard, 2018. *Photo by author.*

If people could grow one crop, I think a lot of people would pick corn, but they weren't allowed to grow corn in the past. Now they are, so it kind of changed the whole vibe of the garden. People really like it. I think it's bringing out new people too, "Wow, I want to get a plot, too!" So we've had a lot of people in the past few months.

A lot of people [in the neighborhood] *used to grow corn in their yards, in their ranches. Everybody likes to grow it, not just for the corn but for the leaves.*

Everyone just loves it, to be able to grow food and hand out food to their friends and neighbors. Some of the Colonia elders are there, growing a lot of berries and giving them to the kids. I think everyone's just grateful that it's there. Everyone wants more space; they have pretty large plots. And we have the communal area in the back. In the back corner we thought, "Hey, let's grow a pumpkin patch!" So we worked with the gardeners there. They volunteered and donated supplies and seeds, and some of the elders there, who have been growing corn their whole lives, were just like, "Oh, here's how you do it," and they would show everyone how to plant the pumpkin. In between the pumpkin you plant the corn. So it's kind of a cool layout,

Community garden seen from the end of Hayes Street, La Colonia, Oxnard, 2018. *Photo by author.*

it's kind of an old milpa [ancient Yucatan companion-planting technique], *planting the corn and the pumpkins together.*

It seems like there's a lot more participating now, too, these days. I think they like to recreate there and just kind of be there to spend time. It's different now because before, everything had to be below three feet; it just didn't feel like a garden. But now there's all this corn and sunflowers....I think a lot more people are just spending time in there and going out there and gardening more.

EL POLLO [THE CHICKEN]

Growing your own food was essential to survival in the Colonia for most of the twentieth century. Until the 1950s and 1960s, many families in the barrio still didn't have refrigeration, so fresh meat was scarce. They relied on what they could grow and what they could keep in the icebox to sustain them. Bob Herrera remembers the days of the icehouse:

Children with grandmother on porch, La Colonia, Oxnard, August 6, 1936. *Courtesy of Martha Muñoz Rodriguez.*

You know dónde está *la Rescue Mission? Over by the railroad tracks? That was the ice company. Right next to Stokely's. You would see the guys with the refrigerator trucks. The motors didn't exist yet. So they had the Union Ice company, they used to break up the ice. Then they would put it on top of the truck so the food wouldn't spoil.*

Did we eat fresh meat? Here's a joke:

One day, my Grandpa Manuel, he told me, "Véngase mijo, es domingo! Venga para acá, vamos a comer pollo ahora." [Come over, son, it's Sunday! Come over because we're going to eat chicken.] *In those days, it was very expensive because they didn't have the meatpacking houses, you know? So whenever they got some meat, it was a big deal!* "Vamos a hacer mole. Van a matar cinco pollos o quien sabe que." [We're going to make mole. We'll kill five chickens or whatever.] *Because everybody was so poor.*

So then I went. And he served me a plate of beans! He called that "pollo!" *Pero the beans were good....*

When we were working, my mom would cook us all kinds of different, good food. Tacos, ándale. *People then were so creative that sometimes they would open the hood of the truck, where the engine is? They would put the* taquitos arriba [the little tacos on top]. *Oh, they were so good! They would get hot and crispy, crunchy.* Que *fast-food?* Ni que nada.

Later, Bob's father built Boy's Market. Bob and his relatives, the Cabral family, became business owners, and though the work was just as hard, the food got a bit of an upgrade—at least for most of the family. Eddie Cabral Jr. remembers:

I feel like we were a little privileged, as business owners in Colonia, honestly. I mean, I was raised on steak and eggs! Because we had a grocery store, we didn't grow up on beans like the previous generation. But I remember my father would still eat cabeza de chivo [goat's head]. *Oh, man! Grandma used to make it for him. My dad would eat it, but I would say, "No way, ain't gonna happen!" I couldn't stand that. They would eat the cheeks and everything! Or* lengua [tongue]. *I didn't like that either. We were fortunate from that perspective; we always had meat to eat.*

Bob and Eddie Sr., Eddie Jr.'s father, were close and shared a taste for the older dishes: "The Cabral family is related to me through my dad's sister. *A mi si me gusta mucha la lengua!* [I really like tongue a lot!] Because, after all, what do the *animalitos* eat? *Puro zacate verde.* [Only green grass.]"

WHY SANDWICHES?

Sometimes, though, food became a way for the Colonia kids to fit in as they ventured into the outside world. Louis Estrada recalls having an icebox in the 1960s:

I remember they would deliver the block of ice and Grandma would put it on the top of the icebox. Every day. There was a hose that went down into the bucket for the water to drain as the ice melted, and she would empty it out.

I also remember when Grandma would prepare our lunch for school. That was the only time that she would serve us sandwiches. On bread. We were never to take anything Mexicano, *no burritos, nothing like that. I never understood why. She would always have ham sandwiches with lettuce, mayo and she would cut it on a diagonal and wrap it in wax paper and put it in a nice brown paper bag with an apple or a piece of fruit. I always wondered, "Why sandwiches?" We never ate sandwiches in the house, but she always had the sandwich ready for school. I didn't make the connection that she was sending us to fit into an American environment.*

THE *RASPADAS*, THOUGH

For decades, Colonia parents knew that they could get their children to complete almost any chore with the promise of a *raspada* (flavored,

Former site of Ordoñez Candy Store, La Colonia, Oxnard, 2018. *Photo by author.*

shaved ice in a cone) from the Ordoñez Candy Store. Many know the rumor that a large confection company had once tried to purchase the recipes for the delicious flavored syrups that the family matriarch made herself, but she would never sell. "Ordoñez, they made the best *raspadas* on Earth!" declares Martha Muñoz Rodriguez. Ofelia Cabral agrees, "They used to sell the best raspadas at the Ordoñez Candy Store! But they were *really* the best."

Ofelia Rodriguez recalls how her father would recruit help from the neighborhood kids when extra hands were needed:

> *When it rained, our yard would flood. So my dad would go to the beach and get sand to soak up all the water. The kids in the neighborhood would help spread the sand all over the yard, and then Dad rewarded them with a* raspada *each. They had the best recipe for the* raspadas. *They were ten cents.*
>
> *It was a poor life but not "dirt poor," as they say. It was a good life.*

WE WENT THROUGH HELL AND BACK

There are two things that come up in all conversations about the Colonia. The first is that people will always tell you what street they grew up on, whether it was one of the "number streets" (First, Second) or one of the "president streets" (Garfield, Grant, Roosevelt). Just the *name* of the street imparts a world of information about what kind of activities that person enjoys, who their friends were and how they made their living.

The second thing a Colonia native will never forget to tell you is how much they love their family.

Manuel Muñoz is very open about how much his sisters mean to him:

I was born in '39, according to history, on Second Street [laughs]. 514 East Second Street, between Garfield and Roosevelt. In the old days, it was just me and my sister Bea and my sister Lulu; [Lulu] passed away. The three of us, we went through hell and back.

Now, my family….My baby sister, she's incredible. Martha was my father's dream come true. I love her a lot. Look, people get sickness, illnesses, you don't know whether you're going to make it or not, people pass away. Within ten years, I went to the hospital for pneumonia three times. But my sisters Lupe and Martha, they call me constantly to see how I'm doing. I'm having surgery soon, and they want to know when and where, all that. They're concerned, you know.

Muñoz family house party, La Colonia, Oxnard, late 1950s. *Courtesy of Martha Muñoz Rodriguez.*

Muñoz family having fun,
La Colonia, Oxnard, 1940s.
*Courtesy of Martha Muñoz
Rodriguez.*

PIN CURL PARTY

Manuel's "baby sister," Martha Muñoz Rodriguez, recalls how having so many cousins around meant that there were always people to have fun with:

> *Now, if you ever went to a pin curl party! In back of this house, on the property, we had a smaller house. So we used to have pin curl parties with my sisters and my cousins. We would do each other's hair.*
>
> *We used to wear the little pajamas with the little bloomer pants. I wore them too* [laughs].

Muñoz family pin curl party, La Colonia, Oxnard, early 1960s. *Courtesy of Martha Muñoz Rodriguez.*

El Travieso

When Cesar Chavez first came to La Colonia as a boy, his immediate family was all he had; his siblings were his playmates. He remembers those first days in the barrio in *Cesar Chavez: Autobiography of La Causa*:

> *My dad was just bringing in some furniture with his brother Valeriano and his sister Carmen, Frank Quintero's mother. When we went inside, I saw a socket without a bulb hanging from the ceiling. I climbed on the bare bed springs to see how it worked, then called my brother. "Hey, Rookie, look at that. Put your finger in there. It tickles you." After Richard put his finger in the socket, I pulled the chain, and he let out a yell. The shock really scared him. When I was small, I was a* travieso—*a prankster. I didn't know I was mean, but Richard has told me that I was.*

Barnacles in the Attic

Many families in La Colonia built their own homes, or at least did their own renovations, even with very little formal education or training. Ruben Espinoza's house on Hayes Street was built by his father.

My family came in maybe '38 or '39. My dad built the house himself. It's hard to believe, but I can believe it because one day I was up in the attic. There were barnacles on some of the beams. I asked my mom, "How come there's barnacles stuck on the wood up here?" And my mom said, "Well, after the rains your dad would go to the ocean, because a lot of driftwood would come up on the shore. He would pick up the best ones and bring them home. He used them to build this house." I couldn't believe it—barnacles and seashells stuck up there in the attic.

It's amazing that he somehow learned carpentry and plumbing and all that. Someone told me that Dad used to look at the Sears catalog, the plumbing section, and study the pipes and figure out what he needed and how it worked. Of course, at that time everything was galvanized or cast iron—pretty heavy. With cast iron, he had to use lead for the joints. He did a lot. I think from him, I observed the way he used tools so later on when

Boy smoking behind old Colonia home with exterior plumbing, Oxnard, 1930s. *Courtesy of Martha Muñoz Rodriguez.*

I was a homeowner, I could do things myself. Of course, now you have YouTube and all that.

Dad even used to do some of his own car repairs. He put a pit in our side yard. It was about six feet deep. It was like a big grave. He would get in there and move the car over the pit so he could work on it. Once, when I was ten or twelve, I was walking around having fun with a big box over my head, and I fell into it. I was crying and yelling, and nobody could hear me! Finally, my aunt, who happened to live next door, she heard me and called out, "Where are you? Dónde estás?" She saw the pit and the box moving and pulled me out.

We had indoor plumbing, as far as I remember. My dad built a shower out of concrete. He built everything; it was amazing what he did with what he had. We had the one bathroom with the shower [for eleven people]. *We all shared rooms. We had bunk beds. My older brother was on the top; I'd thump the bottom of the bed sometimes when I was mad at him. It was fun. The girls always wanted to be by themselves. They would lock the doors so the boys couldn't get in. So the way we would get even later on was that when they started having boyfriends coming around, we'd shoo them away and say the girls weren't home.*

WE HAD BUCKETS ALL OVER THE HOUSE WHEN IT RAINED

Like some of her neighbors, Martha Muñoz Rodriguez was born in a house that had been moved to La Colonia.

They brought the old house from Hueneme or Camarillo in the 1930s. The man that my dad used to work for, he brought it to my dad, and he moved it here for about $150. I guess they had to do all the plumbing and stuff. My mom and dad had to put a down payment on the property of $25. I have the receipt!

The old house had a big Christmas tree in the front yard. We used to put lights on it, but then people used to take the lights. We had a little house in the back, and my tía used to live back there.

By the time I came along, the old house had a bathroom, water and electricity, only we had buckets all over the house when it rained. My mom said, "I'm not going to fix this house!" So we knocked it down and put in a new house in the 1960s.

Children playing with Jose Muñoz in the shade of the palm tree planted by Anita Muñoz, La Colonia, Oxnard, early 1980s. *Courtesy of Martha Muñoz Rodriguez.*

When they put in the new house, my mom planted a palm tree. It grew so big we had to take it down. They had to close the street so we could knock it down.

THE ALLEYS

The streets in La Colonia are very narrow, and there were no sidewalks until well after World War II. So the territory of the Colonia kids was the network of alleys that ran between most of the streets. All the backyards emptied onto the alleys, so adults could keep a bit of an eye on the children as they completed the many chores that could only be done by a grown-up. The Colonia alleys were the scene of many adventures. They were the first place many kids headed the moment school was out. For Corinne Estrada in the 1960s, returning back to the alley after a long afternoon at Santa Clara School was her favorite part of the day:

All you had to do was go out in the alley after school and everybody was there, all the kids just looking for each other. The backyards were all connected by the alley. My brother had a red bike and I had a blue one. We would go out, and all the boys and girls would choose teams and we would race around the block in a relay on our bikes.

One day, my sister and I were supposed to race each other, but we conspired together. When we got on the bikes, we just kept going; we didn't come back! We ended up at the end of the Colonia, by the lemon orchard, and we decided to go trash picking. We saw this purse that was on top of a trash can. When we went to investigate, this man came out of the orchard. He looked disheveled, scary. He came out and was trying to get over to us, and I said to my sister, "Let's go!" She was younger, so she was struggling because she could barely reach the pedals on the bike. We finally got some momentum, and he started running after us! My sister was only five, and she just barely escaped his grasp. It was pretty scary. We saw a lot of stuff like that.

It was strange how, without thinking, I would experience going from our world and crossing the railroad tracks to go to school. Going from a place where you had outhouses and were playing in the street and you'd get dirty running everywhere, then you'd cross over the tracks and you'd never see kids playing in the street. They were playing in their backyards or in their houses! We were always out of the house, on the sidewalk or in the alley.

Even though we had friends outside of the Colonia, at Santa Clara School, nobody ever came to our house. It was not encouraged. Grandma used to call anybody from the outside mancuernas [dumbbells].

The Virgin Adorned with Ribbons

Ofelia Rodriguez recalls the games she played in the alleys and streets of La Colonia:

I still can't figure out how we played some of those games that we played!
There was La Chancla Meada [The Urine-Soaked Flip-Flop or Slipper]. *I don't remember how it went, what led up to it. All I remember was that we had this old* chancla. *You'd pick it up and say something, then you'd throw it up and shout* "La Chancla Meada!" *and somebody would chase you at that point. Kind of like "duck-duck-goose," but it was not in a circle, because you had to have the freedom to run in any direction.*
There was also El Gallo Encantado [The Enchanted Rooster]…*or* La Virgen Con Listónes [The Virgin Adorned with Ribbons].

From left: Martha Muñoz Rodriguez; her mother, Anita Ortiz Muñoz; and a cousin. La Colonia, Oxnard, late 1960s. *Courtesy of Martha Muñoz Rodriguez.*

"Knock! Knock! Knock!"
"Quien es?" [Who is it?]
"La Virgen es. " [It's the Virgin (as in the Virgin Mary).]
"Qué quieres?" [What do you want?]
"Un listón. " [A ribbon.]
"De que color?" [What color ribbon?]
"Amarillo!" [Yellow!]
Everybody had a color, right? Then that person would chase someone.
It was great. Not always, but we were able to adapt and make it a good life.

TINY SWORDS

Ofelia's husband, Fred Rodriguez, was born in 1945 and grew up on Garfield Street, near the lemon orchard, on the same block where Cesar Chavez had once lived.

> *I wonder if the other kids, across the railroad tracks, if they got to go out and play in the street at night. The end of our street, Garfield, was the lemon orchard. So our parents felt safe.*

48

Whenever we would see a car coming, everybody would say, "Stop!" and go to the sidewalk. And the cars were very good about that; they would slow down because they knew us.

We didn't have a playground; we had the lemon orchard. And we had the railroad track. You could put a penny down, in time, you know—we wouldn't endanger ourselves. You'd go back and try to find your flat penny. Or a nail, you could make tiny swords with them.

I remember going to the lemon orchard. We had one eucalyptus tree that somebody had made a platform in. Some friends of mine, Al Rascon and Manuel Gonzalez, we grew up there. We'd put down a penny or a nail, climb up on the platform and just wait for the train to come by.

INCINERATING MAKES STRANGE BEDFELLOWS

Fred's wife, Ofelia, remembers how each of their mothers dealt with the cramped conditions of La Colonia:

My husband's mother was a very strong lady, very stubborn. His family lived behind ours, cater-corner, on Garfield Street, when we were kids.

In the old days, you could burn your own trash in the back. My mother had this big barrel that she would burn her trash in, always on the same day of the week. Monday was wash day. Tuesday was ironing day and so on. So my mom would always wash our clothes on Mondays. And his mom would always burn her trash on Monday. Because they lived behind us, the smoke would always come over and get into our clean clothes.

So my mother went over and asked if she would please not burn her trash on Mondays because my mom had nine kids, so her week was planned out. His mom? She refused. Not only that, but she would burn more *trash! I remember when my husband and I started dating, my tía said, "Oh, if your mother only knew whose side you're on!"*

LA TINA

Martha Muñoz Rodriguez shares a photo her mother kept faithfully for decades. Joined by her brother Manuel, they explain the photo's painful origin:

This photo is of our family member Ernestina that passed away when she fell in a hot tina [large, metal tub used for several purposes, such as laundry] *of water. Standing are her Aunt Paula Dorado (mother of Manuel Dorado, longtime fire chief of La Colonia), Pablo Ortiz and his wife, Manuela Ortiz* [the girl's parents].

Our parents were compadres *to our great-uncle Pablo and Manuela Ortiz. Pablo was the uncle of our mother, Anita Ortiz Muñoz.*

The awful accident was reported in the *Press-Courier*:

Little Ernestina Ortiz, three and a half-year old Oxnard Mexican child, succumbed to second and third degree burns at 3:21 yesterday afternoon after having fallen into a tub full of boiling wash water in the backyard of her parents' Colonia Garden home yesterday morning, Coroner Ted Mayr revealed today. According to Mayr, 80 percent of the child's body was scalded when she fell backward into the water. The parents are Mr. and Mrs. Pablo Ortiz of 115 North Grant street, Colonia Garden.

Mayr reported the little girl was playing near the tub of boiling water and had a piece of canvas in her arms. The child tripped over the canvas and fell backward into the water. The child's mother, Manuela Ortiz, rushed to the tub when she heard the little girl's screams and picked her pain-wracked daughter from the boiling water.

The child was rushed to the county hospital where she was treated for the critical burns. Despite a frantic effort to save her life, the child died late yesterday afternoon, Mayr stated. There is to be no inquest into the death.

A sad footnote to this tragedy is the article's statement that "the child was rushed to the county hospital." Oxnard's main hospital, the old St. John's Hospital, was hardly a mile from the scene of the accident. In his book *Strategies of Segregation*, Dr. David G. Garcia notes a "record of racial exclusion at St. John's Hospital before World War II." It may have been the case that, because Mexican Americans were not admitted to St. John's, the Ortiz family would have had to take their severely injured daughter from the bumpy, unpaved streets of La Colonia all the way to the county hospital in Ventura, a thirty-minute trip at the time.

From left: Paulita Dorado, Pablo Ortiz, Manuela Ortiz and Angelena Ortiz (partly out of shot) at the burial of Ernestina Ortiz, Oxnard, 1941. *Courtesy of Martha Muñoz Rodriguez.*

THAT'S WHAT YOU DO, BECAUSE THIS IS FAMILY

With all of the cousins, *tías* and *tíos* (aunts and uncles), *compadres* and *comadres* (godparents), those who have Colonia roots often think of the entire barrio as family.

Walking into local businesses or church functions, it's quite common for one to be addressed, no matter their age, as "*Mija*" or "*Mijo*" ("My Daughter" or "My Son"), even by people who are no relation whatsoever. This lends a familial atmosphere to all events, as Dr. Elvia Estrella recalls, especially the sad ones:

> *I remember my first funeral in the Colonia; I had to be in kindergarten. I learned how to pray the second part of the Hail Mary because we would always do the* novenario [prayers said over nine days when someone has died, usually in a relative's home]. *There was the rosary and the* pan dulce…*everybody was there. I remember being on my knees and praying* "Santa Maria, Madre de Dios…" [Holy Mary, Mother of God].
>
> *There was a collection, and I remember my dad being very generous because whoever passed was from La Colonia.* [My father] *worked three jobs to be able to afford our house payment on the West Side. And he was putting a fifty-dollar bill in the collection. I looked and thought, "Wow, that's a lot of money!" But it was one of those things my dad and mom always taught us: "That's what you do, because this is family."*
>
> *It sounds sad, but I almost looked forward to those* novenarios. *"Okay, after I pray the rosary, I'm gonna get some* pan dulce *and I can play outside in the dark!" Because where we lived, even though it was the "better" neighborhood, we couldn't go out to play because there was no one else there like us.*

CHAPTER 3

CALLED TO SERVE

La Colonia Joins the Ranks

Throughout the twentieth century, men and women of the Colonia did their part to serve their country. During World War II, hundreds of Oxnard citizens of Japanese descent were sent to internment camps, while Mexican Americans from the Colonia, like their African American neighbors, were sent off to fight in segregated units. Later, during the Korean and Vietnam Wars, many more Colonia kids put their lives on the line for their country. Service took them far from the barrio, and many formed lifelong careers and relationships.

THE LAST ONE TO SEE ROMEO ALIVE

Joe Anguiano's brother Andy served in World War II. He relates a story of how his brother encountered an old friend from the Colonia a world away from home.

> *My brother Andy was drafted into the army around '41. He served with the 179th Infantry Division. He served under General Patton. Andy served in North Africa and the invasion of Sicily. He was wounded going into Rome.*
>
> *In the service, he had a good friend of his who was from the Colonia,* un muchacho *named Romeo Ramirez.*
>
> *When Andy was wounded in Sicily, he saw a chaplain. Andy asked him about Romeo. The chaplain said, "Yes, I know him." Andy said, "He's*

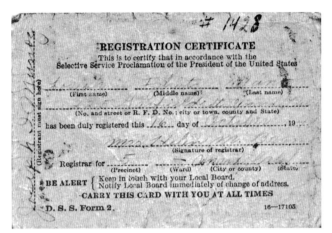

Left: Selective Service registration card of Jose Muñoz, Oxnard, 1940s. *Courtesy of Martha Muñoz Rodriguez.*

Below: Jesus Lopez, *right*, with his compadre Hilario in uniform, Oxnard, 1940s. *Courtesy of Lupe Lopez Lujan.*

a good friend of mine from the States." And the chaplain said, "Well, if you'll still be here this time tomorrow, I'll bring Romeo to see you." Andy and Romeo met for a while that day, sharing stories about back home before they had to ship out again. This time they were going into Rome; the divisions were advancing. My brother was wounded again and ended up in the hospital. Again, he inquired after Romeo, saying he had a friend in the division and asked if they knew where he was. They told him Romeo was killed, and Andy felt real bad. So Andy was the last one from back home to see Romeo alive. [Romeo Ramirez was posthumously decorated with the Bronze Star and the Purple Heart, which were sent back to La Colonia to his widow and adopted son.] *My brother was broken-hearted because they were good friends.*

Meanwhile, our mother had cancer. Since he'd been wounded twice, Andy couldn't return to the front, so he made his way home. But he was only in New York when our mother passed. We didn't know yet that he was in the States or even if he knew what had happened. So when our mother died, we buried her. We didn't know we could have waited for Andy. The next day, we got word that he was still in New York. It's one of those things, it happens.

HE WAS A FUNNY GUY

Manuel Muñoz remembers seeing his neighbors sent off to the internment camps during World War II:

When the war started against Japan, I remember there was this friend of ours, he became the mayor of Oxnard one time, his name was Takasugi. He was a funny guy. They deported him to a camp, right about 1942, I would say.

During the time of Pearl Harbor, we had four uncles in the army. One was in North Africa, one was in Europe, one went to Korea and the other one in France. You know the stars they put in the window? At that time, it would mean you had somebody serving in the military.

Shortly after the war, though he was still a boy, Manuel's friends started getting in trouble during the unrest that was beginning to creep into the Colonia. Young Muñoz made a life-changing decision:

To get away from all that stuff, I joined the Boy Scouts. That's where I met Adolfo Camarillo because he was a member of the Elks Club. They sponsored us, our troop, #203, in the Colonia. Our meeting was in a navy Quonset. I was a Boy Scout for many years, and then I became an Explorer Scout. I joined the Order of the Arrow and learned how to survive out in the wilderness, eating snakes and berries or whatever. We'd make traps for any kind of animal you can eat and survive, like rabbits.

Then roundabout 1956, I got lonely because all my buddies were gone. I used to think, "Where the heck are they?" So I became a member of the National Guard. I told my mother and dad, I was sixteen so they had to sign a parent's consent. So from 1956 until 1999, I was in the National Guard. For forty-five years, I was protecting the State of California.

For Muñoz, the National Guard played a large role in every aspect of his life: "I retired from the National Guard as a staff sergeant. You'd meet people from all walks of life: lawyers, cooks, doctors….But my life was very happy. No regrets about anything."

You Can't Work on Me

Fred Rodriguez was the first in his family to go to college.

> *I went to Ventura College, but then I took a summer off to work because I couldn't afford it, I couldn't afford my books. Because I took that time off, I lost my student status and was drafted into the army. I went to Paris for nine months, then to Germany for nine months, then to Denmark, where I was a medic.*
>
> *I was an army dental hygienist in Paris. One time, a southern man came in. He asked me if I was a Latino, and I said, "Yes." He said, "You can't work on me." Then the dentist, who was Jewish, came and said, "I can't work on you if you don't let him work on you." The man left.*
>
> *I had to walk through a forest every day. I liked it. I would buy a baguette and a liter of milk….When I came back, I had the GI Bill, but it was held up for three months. So I went to work at the Ventura County Hospital* [before finishing school].

It Became a Career

Ruben Espinoza never imagined that he would go to college. A drafting teacher at Oxnard High School mentioned it to him and then took him to the counselor and demanded they help the boy get into a good school. It wasn't always easy, but eventually, Ruben graduated from Cal Poly. Unfortunately, he was finishing college at an inopportune time in our nation's history.

> *That was when the Vietnam War was happening. I thought, "My God, I'm going to get drafted." One of my roommates got drafted, and someone suggested, "Hey, why don't you join the reserves? It'll keep you out of the draft." So I did. I joined during my junior year.*
>
> *We would go to the airport where they had the federal reserve meetings. During one of those meetings, the officer said, "Espinoza, you're a college*

guy, right? You should apply for officer's school." I asked, "What's that?" He said, "Well, when you graduate, you can go to officer's school. You'll make a lot more money. If you're going to be in the service anyway, you might as well make the best money." I said, "Okay! Sign me up!"

At the end of my junior year of college, they sent me to Rhode Island. I'd never been out of Colonia! I was on an airplane flying to the East Coast. What an experience! I was looking out the windows, everything was so green, lakes and trees. I was used to California, dry hills. After I graduated [I went back east again] *and finished officer's school. I have a degree in math. I was stationed in a navy yard in Washington, D.C. I was in active duty for two years. It became a career. I enjoyed it.*

Discrimination was more subtle then, but I could sense it. When people would call me, they'd say, "Juan, come here!" or "Jose, come here!" They knew my name was Ruben. Things like that. But mostly I was well respected, I enjoyed my time in the service.

…When you live in a place like Colonia, and everybody's the same, you don't think about it. That's just the way it is; you just live. But it's when you get exposed to different things, it opens your eyes to possibilities. That's why I think it's important for any young kids, any age really, to get exposed to different environments. That way they know what they'd like a lot sooner than if they were never exposed to a variety of things.

The Unbelievable True Story of Al Rascon

Ruben Espinoza and Al Rascon lived on the same block of Hayes Street in La Colonia, near the lemon orchard. Ruben remembers:

He was my neighbor for quite a few years; we were in the Boy Scouts together. It was funded by the Elks Club. I remember that he loved Boy Scouts, I guess the discipline and the procedures.…

I think the Boy Scouts kept us out of any delinquency problems. The meeting place was just around the corner from us, in the Quonset huts. We went on camping trips, field trips.…I earned the Eagle Scout award. Adolfo Camarillo made the presentation. I'm very thankful it kept us occupied and taught us, showed us the oceans and sierras, and kept us off of Cooper Road, where some of the bad stuff was going on.

We did goofy things in those days! Somehow, we figured out how to make a smoke bomb. If you threw them hard enough, they would start to

Bruce Ingraham	Fred Clay	Joe Espinosa	Sharon Dawson	Tom Dunnion
Milene Laurent	Caroline Colen	Carolyn Sheppard	Cindy Clemens	Marion Ingrahan
Carole Moss		Al Rascon	Dan Dawes	Betty Carlson

Al Rascon, *center bottom*, in his Oxnard High School revue, 1963. *Courtesy of Bungalow Productions.*

burn and fizz and smoke. We did that once in the Quonset hut at one of the Scout meetings when there was nothing going on. The place filled up with smoke, and we got scared! We ran and opened the windows. It really scared us; we thought the place was going to burn down.

Al was my neighbor, and he eventually moved out of La Colonia to the other side of town. I guess more than anybody else I remember, he liked to put on that uniform. As you know, he received the Medal of Honor! Amazing. I read some of the things he went through. I remember thinking, "Little Al Rascon, my God."

The story truly *is* amazing. Alfredo Velazquez Rascon was born in Chihuahua, Mexico, in 1945, the only child of Alfredo and Andrea Rascon. Alfredo was a toddler when his family moved to La Colonia. When he graduated from Oxnard High School in 1963 and enlisted in the United States Army, Rascon was still not a naturalized citizen of the United States. He did basic and medical training, and by 1965, Al Rascon was in Vietnam. As the following citation attests, it was the beginning of a staggering military career:

Specialist Four Alfred Rascon, distinguished himself by a series of extraordinarily courageous acts on March 16, 1966, while assigned as a medic to the Reconnaissance Platoon, Headquarters Company, 1st Battalion (Airborne), 503rd Infantry, 173rd Airborne Brigade (Separate).

While moving to reinforce its sister battalion under intense enemy attack, the Reconnaissance Platoon came under heavy fire from a numerically superior enemy force. The intense enemy fire from crew-served weapons and grenades severely wounded several point squad soldiers. Specialist Rascon, ignoring directions to stay behind shelter until covering fire could be provided, made his way forward.

He repeatedly tried to reach the severely wounded point machine-gunner laying on an open enemy trail, but was driven back each time by the withering fire.

Disregarding his personal safety, he jumped to his feet, ignoring flying bullets and exploding grenades to reach his comrade. To protect [the comrade] *from further wounds,* [Rascon] *intentionally placed his body between the soldier and enemy machine guns, sustaining numerous shrapnel injuries and a serious wound to the hip. Disregarding his serious wounds he dragged the larger soldier from the fire-raked trail.*

Hearing the second machine-gunner yell that he was running out of ammunition, Specialist Rascon, under heavy enemy fire crawled back to the wounded machine-gunner, stripping him of his bandoleers of ammunition, giving them to the [other, non-wounded] *machine-gunner who continued his suppressive fire.*

Specialist Rascon, fearing the abandoned machine gun, its ammunition and spare barrel could fall into enemy hands made his way to retrieve them. On the way, he was wounded in the face and torso by grenade fragments, but disregarded these wounds to recover the abandoned machine gun, ammunition and spare barrel items, enabling another soldier to provide added suppressive fire to the pinned-down squad.

In searching for the wounded, he saw the point grenadier being wounded by small arms fire and grenades being thrown at him....Specialist Rascon reached and covered him with his body, absorbing the blasts from the exploding grenades, and saving the soldier's life, but sustaining additional wounds to his [own] *body.*

While making his way to the wounded point squad leader, grenades were hurled at the sergeant. Again, in complete disregard for his own life, [Rascon] *reached and covered the sergeant with his* [own] *body, absorbing the full force of the grenade explosions. Once more Specialist Rascon was critically wounded by shrapnel, but disregarded his own wounds to continue to search and aid the wounded.*

Severely wounded, he remained on the battlefield, inspiring his fellow soldiers to continue the battle. After the enemy broke contact, he disregarded aid for himself, instead treating the wounded and directing their evacuation. Only after being placed on the evacuation helicopter did he allow aid to be given to him.

Specialist Rascon was so wounded that when he finally accepted aid, after first making sure all the other wounded had been attended to, he was also administered the last rites. It took months of recovery in a Japanese hospital, but unbelievably, Alfredo Velazquez Rascon survived. The following year, he became a naturalized United States citizen.

For his "extraordinary valor," he was nominated for the Medal of Honor, the single highest personal service decoration that can be awarded. However, somehow the nomination was lost, and instead Rascon was awarded the Silver Star. In the years that followed, Alfred Rascon finished his education and continued his impressive military career, eventually reaching the rank of lieutenant colonel.

In 1985, when his comrades discovered Rascon had never received the Medal of Honor, they nominated him again. They were told by the Pentagon that it was hopeless, that too much time had passed. But they persisted, eventually gaining the support of a congressman who, in turn, brought it to the attention of the president of the United States.

Finally, after nearly thirty-five years, Lieutenant Colonel Alfred Velazquez Rascon was presented with the Medal of Honor by President Bill Clinton.

Later, under President George W. Bush, Lieutenant Colonel Rascon became director of the Selective Service System from 2001 until 2003. He served in Afghanistan and Iraq. In gratitude for his service, the army renamed its training school for medics after him. The Alfred V. Rascon School of Combat Medicine is located in Kentucky, at Fort Campbell.

He is retired and lives in Maryland.

Oxnard High School senior photo of Lieutenant Colonel Alfred Rascon, 1963. *Courtesy of Bungalow Productions.*

CHAPTER 4

WORK

La Pisca, but So Much More

For the third article in his "Colonia" series, Don W. Martin undertook the task of describing a working day in the barrio.

> *"Colonia's Workers Rise and Retire with the Sun"*
> *At 5:30 am, while most citizens of Oxnard are still asleep, people begin to gather at the intersection of Hayes Street and Cooper Road.*
>
> *Laborers, carrying sack lunches, walk out of nearby houses and the weather-blackened Hotel Juarez. They gather in groups at the intersection, or meet in two corner cafes, La Michoacana and La Tropicana. Most are Mexican-Americans; a few are Negroes.*
>
> *They sip morning coffee, or eat plates of scrambled eggs, and wait.*
>
> *They are preparing for a unique hiring ceremony, an event which resembles something out of another era as farmers come to draw their field hands for the day.*

The article's purpose was to give *Press-Courier* readers a first glimpse into the daily life of a Colonia resident. Though weii-intentioned, the article failed to chronicle the many kinds of work that Colonia people did to keep the city running. Yes, there was *la pisca* (picking or field work), but there were also the packinghouses, transportation companies and all the businesses needed to support the neighborhood itself.

The Hotel Juarez is largely unchanged from the day it was observed by Don W. Martin, 2018. *Photo by author.*

IF THE LEMONS WEREN'T HEAVY, I WOULD GO TO THE FISH CANNERY

Like many in La Colonia, Martha Muñoz Rodriguez's family résumé is long and impossibly varied. It wasn't all waiting on street corners and sipping coffee.

> *I started picking walnuts at fourteen. My tío Pablo was a foreman at the berry farm, so I worked two years picking strawberries. When I turned sixteen, I went to work at the packinghouse on Third Street. From there, if the lemons weren't heavy, I would go to the fish cannery.*

My mom worked everywhere: Seaboard Lemon, the cannery, the chilería, *Gentry's and the carrot company on Fifth Street, Gumper's.*

My dad always worked in the fields, from picking celery to being a foreman. Even when he was a foreman, he used to work. He felt it was important, that he had to be there. He picked tomatoes and cucumbers, tomates y pepinos. *Those were my favorite. We used to just take our salt shaker for lunch! But then I would get bloody noses; I guess the heat was not my best friend.*

Generations of Colonia kids remember "Miss Marta" very fondly. She was the beloved janitor at Ramona Elementary, where she herself had once been a student. It wasn't much of a commute. The house her family had occupied since the 1930s was right across the street from the school. She remembers:

I worked at Ramona School from 1983 until 2014. The district retired me because I have an artificial hip. They said they were afraid one of the kids would knock me down. You know, because they'd run up and hug you. I had no trouble with any of them, and they knew not to mess with me either!

INSTEAD OF COFFEE IN A THERMOS, WINE

Martha's big brother Manuel Muñoz remembers another job their father held.

My father and two of his brothers used to work at the sugar factory. When I was old enough to walk all the way out to the factory, I'd take lunch out to them.

My mother would pack a lunch of tacos and beans and rice. Instead of coffee in a thermos, it had a bottle of wine in it. How can you take a bottle of wine to the sugar factory? That's what they had for lunch. Isn't that something?

But you know what? That's what they call surviving. Survival means any kind of work would do. Dad worked in the sugar factory before he became a rancher. He worked on a ranch down the way, Jack Ecoff Ranch.

THAT TIME IT SNOWED

Like everyone in Oxnard on January 11, 1949, Manuel Muñoz will never forget "that time it snowed." For the workers of La Colonia, the snow was certainly a fun novelty, but it was also just another very cold day at work for many men and women who were ill prepared for the chill.

In January of '49, it snowed. That's my dad in the all-around tractor. My dad was standing up and our cousin Phillip Castillo was driving it. You can see it in the background, the white snow. They were really dressed up [to try and fight the cold]. *It was my oldest sister's birthday, January 11, 1949. It was maybe about four or five inches. Just enough to say, "Hooray! Hooray!"*

Above: Jose Muñoz and Philip Castillo work in the snow, Oxnard, January 11, 1949. *Courtesy of Martha Muñoz Rodriguez.*

Left: Front page of the newspaper, Oxnard, January 11, 1949. *Image from* Oxnard Press-Courier.

STRAWBERRIES? I LOVE STRAWBERRIES!

As one of nine children, Ofelia Rodriguez saw not only her father but also her siblings go to work in the fields.

My parents pushed education, so every one of us nine kids finished high school. Then the three oldest had to go to work to help support the rest of us. So, if I hadn't had such a large family and been one of the last ones born, I probably would have gone to work in the fields in the summer. But I didn't have to because by the time I was old enough to work in the fields, my older siblings were working and contributing to the household.

I remember one time, my brother Ruben and a couple of my sisters were going to work in the strawberries. I really wanted to go, but my dad said, "No, you're too young. Maybe later." When they came back that day, they were all chorreados [stained]*! Their knees were mushy because of the stooping. So no, I never asked again. Because I thought it was going to be fun, right? "Strawberries? I love strawberries!"*

THEY'D PAY WITH WATCHES

Ofelia's brother Ruben, who had come back from the strawberry fields that day, has vivid memories of the many jobs to be done in La Colonia.

My mom was a homemaker from Mexico. I had six sisters and two brothers—big family. My dad was farm labor for a long time.

Dad liked to play poker; I'm told that he was good at it. So the owner of the card room he used to go to said, "Well, you're making more money than I am, how would you like to be pit boss?" So he ran the card room for the guy. Eventually, he was able to buy it out.

Little by little, Dad no longer worked in the fields; he made his living running the poker room. Eventually, he expanded across the street and put in a pool hall with a bar, and he gave me a job there when I was in high school. I was a janitor. Let me tell you, I never wanted to do it again. It was terrible!

In time, the city outlawed the clubs, except at places like the Elks Club. You could go there if you were a member. [During this era, the Oxnard Elks Club was strictly segregated.] *So that basically shut Dad down, but he was able to buy a liquor license and opened up a liquor store on south Oxnard*

Boulevard. That's where he made his living. He supported us, and with no education at all! You have to give the guy credit. He was smart enough to get the right people around him, you know, accountants and people to help him run the businesses. He had the same kind of deal in Carpinteria, too, a pool room and bar. He ran both the businesses at the same time.

I worked at the liquor store, 101 Drive-In Liquor, stocking beer and candy. My oldest brother Arthur had learned auto upholstery at a trade school and was working in LA. When my dad died, Arthur came back and ran the liquor store business with us. It was a big sacrifice for him, but without him, the family would've gone under.

Eventually, we did sell it to a gentleman who had other liquor stores in the area. He renamed it. I don't think it's a liquor store anymore.

When my dad passed away, we went through his things, and there were all these cigar boxes full of watches and jewelry. People would gamble and run out of money, so they'd pay with watches.

AT LUNCH TIME WE'D SIT, STILL HUNCHING OVER

Fred Rodriguez has happy memories of his days working in the fields, though the work was very, very hard.

View of the old lemon packinghouse from outside La Colonia, on Oxnard Boulevard, Oxnard, 2018. *Photo by author.*

The hardest part was doing the short-petal hull. Because it was like this [walks sideways, crossing leg over leg while stooped over] all day. You had tomato plants you had to cut or pull with your hand. So you were hunched over all day long. At lunch time we'd sit, still hunching over. It hurt too much to straighten up. I did that for one whole summer.

Then I picked in the lemon orchards by Oxnard High School. That was nice. There were still braceros *then, and they would sing. You'd hear these guys just singing. It was beautiful! That was really nice, I enjoyed that.*

The hardest thing I remember was that, for the women, there were no bathrooms. So they'd have to go off…and there'd be one woman standing at the edge so nobody would come over.

To pick lemons, you'd have to wear long sleeves, with a leather thing to go over them. You'd get your ladder; it had a stick and a hinge. You'd have to flip it and throw the ladder against the tree so you could get into it.

At lunch time, it was really neat. Somebody was in charge of making a fire; they'd burn the eucalyptus. Then you'd throw your taco on there, and that eucalyptus smell was very soothing. As a matter of fact, whenever we barbecue now, sometimes I'll go and look for some eucalyptus and throw it in. Good memories, in that sense.

I GOT TO LIVE IN A ZOO

Sometimes work was an adventure. Fred recalls a job his mother held over two summers:

When I was in junior high, my mom worked at Jungleland. For two summers, she took me there. Our little apartment there was smaller than most living rooms. But we were right next to Jackie the Third, one of the lions.

Jungleland was an animal theme park in Thousand Oaks, south of Oxnard. It was created to support the Hollywood studios, keeping and training animals used in films and television, including the famous MGM lion and Mr. Ed.

I got to be with the lion tamers and chimpanzee keepers. When I was in high school and people would ask me, "What did you do last summer?" I would always say, "Well, I didn't do anything this summer except work in the strawberries. But when I was in junior high? I got to live in a zoo!" Then they would ask, "What did you do?" I would say, "Oh, I got to go with the lion tamers when they fed their lions at night. I got to be with the butcher, who would get a horse and take him out to the back and shoot him and cut him up. For food, you know, for the lions."

WHERE DID EVERYBODY GO?

Lupe Lujan preferred strawberries over lemons.

My sister Aurora and I used to go pick strawberries. At that time, there were still a lot of braceros. We were the youngest ones there. All of a sudden, you'd hear someone yell, "La migra [immigration]*!" Oh! My sister and I would be looking around, "What's happening? Where did everybody go?" Everyone would be gone. After a while, they would start trickling back in.*

It was still dark when we'd get there, to the field, and people would make their brasas [cooking fires] *to heat up their food. They would always share. It would be so cold, and everyone would be huddled around these little campfires, eating their little breakfast.*

I only lasted in the lemons one day. You'd have to climb the tall, tall ladder, and you had this gunnysack. You had to pick the lemons from the top of the ladder—and there were terrible thorns! Then climb back down the ladder with this heavy sack and walk to the end of the row and dump it into this big wooden crate. And then do it all over again! I thought, "No, I'll go back to the strawberries."

Lemon harvest, Oxnard, 1940s. *Courtesy of Bungalow Productions.*

THREE *PANADERÍAS* AND A *CURANDERA*

The Martinez family had a grandmother with a unique business in the Colonia. "My grandmother Maria Martinez Villareal was a *curandera*," recalls Rachel Martinez Sandoval. A *curandera* is a traditional Mexican healer who would often use herbs, massage and other techniques to help people who didn't always have access to conventional healthcare. Doña Maria had a reputation for being a particularly good *curandera*.

Aurora De la Selva's mother would often take her children to see Doña Maria. "I don't know what she did or how she did it, but I tell you, when we left, we would always feel better!" Doctors and hospitals were reserved for emergencies only.

Ofelia Cabral recalls the Martinezes' grandmother as well:

> *There was a woman* que te sobaba, *she would massage you.*
>
> *Next to that, for a little while, there was Panadería La Azteca. It was across the street from Ochos* [a longtime Colonia watering hole]. *You'd have to climb the stairs. I remember that the* panadería *was upstairs. Of course there was also La Central; it's still there! It's been there over a hundred years.*

Panadería La Central has been serving La Colonia for over a century, Oxnard, 2018. *Photo by author.*

Interior, Panadería La Central, Oxnard, 2018. *Photo by author.*

Exterior, Panadería Lupitas, La Colonia, Oxnard, 2018. *Photo by author.*

Juan Manuel Martinez and Gregorio Martinez of Panadería Lupitas, Oxnard, 2018. *Photo by author.*

Colonia residents often use the barrio's *panaderías* (traditional Mexican bakeries) as reference points throughout the neighborhood. They are an important part of the local culture. Each one has its specialty. Some families might visit up to three *panaderías* on a single Sunday to make sure everyone at the table got their favorite treat.

La Azteca is long gone, but another neighborhood institution, Panadería Lupitas, is still going strong in the heart of the barrio. Starting out as a *paletería* selling frozen treats, it later became a restaurant, which expanded to include the bakery. Panadería Lupitas is still family owned and operated, and it still makes the special miniature *pan dulce* it created years ago for the children in La Colonia's elementary schools.

LA CHILERÍA

Like many women of the Colonia, Ofelia Cabral worked in the *chilería*, the Coastal Valley Canning Company (aka the Ortega plant), processing and packing chiles.

> *The* chilería *was only seasonal. We used to work about ten hours a day for three months out of the year. We'd work with the machines that would*

Colonia women working at the *chilería*, Oxnard, 1962. *Image from* Oxnard Press-Courier.

cover the cans up. So all we had to do was watch that the machines would never run out of lids. We would just stand around, watching the machines and talking, and get paid good money! All the people of the Colonia worked at the chilería. *It was good because you'd earn really good money in a really short time.*

I Started Working When I Was About Ten

Bob Herrera is the embodiment of the Colonia work ethic.

I started working when I was about ten.…My dad started a trucking company in the off-seasons, and they used to haul concrete cinder blocks all over the place. In those days they didn't have forklifts, so there was always a "swamper," which was a person who went along with the driver. They always had to be on time or else they'd get billed for the contractor and his workers having to wait.

It was wonderful. It was hard work! We used to have these rubber gloves. The driver would put the blocks on the end of the bed, and we would have to get them and stack them, nice and straight or else they would tip over. We didn't mind it because when you're a kid, you never feel that anything hurts here or there.

Later, when Bob's family opened Boy's Market, things improved, but there was still much work to do.

It was a blessing because I had a lot of friends my age who didn't know what they wanted to do after they graduated. We didn't have to worry about that because we were already in business. So we'd coast along, just doing our work. We used to stay 'til midnight sometimes, stocking the shelves. We didn't mind it. And Eddie [Cabral] Sr. was great; he was the manager. All of us, along with my brothers Ruben, Carlos and Ben, we had a lot of fun.

Eddie Cabral Jr. also enjoyed his work at the market:

For me as a kid, I saw Bob and my dad, all those guys having a blast in the store. It wasn't even work for these guys, just a lot of awesome memories. And a difference from now: I remember noticing when I was a teenager how Bob and my dad used to know all the families by their names. The whole family, from the youngest kid to the oldest grandfather! Back in those days, we had winos, but they weren't homeless then. They worked but they just had problems.

The people there in the Colonia, it was a great community. It really, really was! I remember the lemon trucking business, seeing all those guys getting off of their trucks on Colonia Road to come into the store, so quick,

Exterior, Boy's Market, La Colonia, Oxnard, 2018. *Photo by author.*

to buy sodas and a beer here and there. Really quick; these guys were hustling! You don't see that too much anymore.

My father was a very hardworking man, Bob's a very hardworking man and I know I am! We all work hard; it's in our blood. My brother and I were always in management, but everyone is very much needed. As a kid, I already knew what I wanted to do, so I was working hard.

Eddie Jr.'s brother Richie also enjoyed the benefits of growing up in the store, but he never took it for granted:

It was great. If we ever wanted candy, we'd just go to Boy's and get one. So many families had businesses, like Bob had the Boy's Market and we had a grocery store and a trucking company after that. So work was very important.

…I think of our family coming from Zacatecas during those [revolution] times; they probably didn't have a lot of money, no car, just the clothes on their back. They came on top of the trains, on top of the boxcars. Five hundred miles—that's unbelievable.

Joe and Rachel

Joe and Rachel Anguiano have been married for over sixty years. On a table in the front room of their house, visitors can see a framed program from the football game they attended on their first date. The couple hailed from Saticoy, a small town about seven miles from La Colonia, but in the 1960s, they became a part of the community when the Department of Labor wanted someone from out of the area to open an office in the barrio.

Rachel Anguiano remembers the occasion pictured here:

> *The Colonia office opened when my son Chris was three, 1967. It was a torn-down building, and Joe himself had to do all the work. He painted it and everything!*
>
> *I always felt at home there. I remember I used to take my kids out to lunch in the Colonia. One time I was walking along with my three kids and there was a woman I knew; she was a realtor. She saw me coming out of the restaurant and she said, "Oh, do you live here now?" Like that was supposed to be putting me down somehow! I said, "No, I don't live here, but my husband has an office here. We love it!"*

Joe's parents ran a store in Saticoy, much like the Cabrals and Bob Herrera did in the Colonia. And like them, the experience of growing up in the neighborhood store gave Joe a deep sense of community and a drive to help

Father Madera, *right*, says a prayer for the founding of the new MAOF office as the Anguianos' young son, *center*, looks on, Oxnard, 1968. *Image from* Oxnard Press-Courier.

others. Joe remembers that when the opportunity to work with the people of La Colonia came along, he and Rachel were very happy to roll up their sleeves and jump in.

I had an office on Cooper Road, the MAOF [Mexican American Opportunity Foundation]. That's where I met so many people from La Colonia that we still know today.

We went to everyone's weddings at Cristo Rey and Guadalupe. They had the Neighborhood Youth Corps, Tom Williams started that, but I worked more with Sr. Camacho from the CSO [Community Service Organization]. We worked together along with Rosa Williams; she worked the new careers program.

Tornicio Morales lived in Moorpark and worked with the lemon workers there. He knew there were a lot of changes going on in Oxnard, that they were taking out a lot of the fields to do building. He thought that the workers there might be kind of lost and would need to find jobs, so he started MAOF in Los Angeles. Mr. Morales got funded through his friend Edward Roybal [co-founder of the CSO]. They got funds through the Department of Labor, and he opened thirteen offices in California [in 1963].

Some people weren't sure about me at first because I was from out of the area; I can understand that. But the MAOF decided they didn't want a local, native resident of the area to run the office.

We were working with anybody that was Hispanic, low-income and wanted to work. We would go into industries like Northrop [aircraft manufacturer] or 3M, IBM and the like and ask if they had any openings for jobs. We paid half of people's wages while they trained so they could afford to do the training.

It wasn't that we just placed them and left them there—no. And it wasn't that the companies were just going to take them on and let them go. They had to commit to keeping them. Northrop at that time was building the shuttles, and we were often placing ladies who had worked in the lemon orchards or the packinghouses of Oxnard. Their hands were very skilled, so when they were working with the fiberglass and plastics, they were better at those tasks than the labor the companies would typically get. So that opened a lot of doors for a lot of people.

We placed a lot of women, like Mrs. [Aurora] Lopez. She did really well at Northrop and 3M. We had another lady, Lily, she worked for 3M and they made a movie of her! They actually went to the field where she used to work to show where'd she come from.

And that's what we needed, for people to go in and do a really good job in such a company. That opened the door for us to place more people. That's how we had foremen and laypeople who were able to advance themselves. We also placed people at Apex. They did a lot of machine-dye work, government contracts. And Semtech [supplier of analog and mixed-signal semiconductors] *had a lot of assembly work, so we placed a lot of people there.*

Sometimes people didn't have a car or didn't have a ride, so they would call me and I would take them to work. In those days, my territory was Thousand Oaks to Santa Barbara.

Later, we hired Al Torres and Fermin Herrera to work in the office. Fermin was in between UCLA and his first teaching jobs. Andres Herrera, his brother, we placed at Northrop through MAOF. So that's how I got to know the Herrera family. I got Andres into Northrop, personnel managing in

Joe Anguiano at the time the first MAOF office was opened in La Colonia, Oxnard, 1960s. *Image from* Oxnard Press-Courier.

Hueneme where they were building barges. Then later, when the MAOF in Oxnard was closing? Andres hired me! I went to work at Northrop, too. That's how I ended up, with only a high school diploma, working in the Northrop personnel office.

In time, I was offered a job at the Department of Employment because I knew so many people and they liked what I was doing. They had a desk for me, they were going to shoot me right in there, but then my dad said I had to come back home and take over the family store. So we went back to Saticoy.

We didn't want to leave the Colonia, but it was family. I should have gone to work at the DOE because it would have been easier—five days, benefits. By the time the kids were in school, I was working sixteen-hour days, seven days a week in the store. But we got all those kids through college! We are so proud of our kids and grandkids.

But those days at the MAOF, they were very special. And yes, we had a lot of people who, later on, would come up to me and thank me. And you know, that was truly rewarding. It really opened the door for a lot of people.

I think that we did a lot of good. Roberto De la Selva and Gene Lujan were a lot of help to me; we developed a real good friendship that lasted. It was a big struggle, but it was worth it, it was rewarding. [Recently] *I worked at the pantry at Project Understanding in Cabrillo Village with*

Joe and Rachel Anguiano, Ventura, 2018. *Photo by author.*

Gene's son, Andres, and he's made a difference with the kids there. When I started there, we were feeding 80 people a month, and within a year, we had doubled that. When I left at the end of the program, we were serving 1,800.

Today, at the pantry in Cabrillo Village, there is a small plaque that commemorates Mr. Anguiano's lifelong work, calling him "San Jose de los Trabajadores" (St. Joseph of the Workers).

Joe and Rachel Anguiano live just outside of Oxnard in Ventura, California.

CHAPTER 5

UNREST, ACTIVISM AND PROGRESS

"Aggressive in Spirit"

A s the Colonia kids became teenagers, crossing the tracks on a daily basis brought new challenges, but it also opened new worlds to them, and there was no going back. Their experiences of Oxnard in the 1950s and 1960s would inspire them to push for progress in a city that had been demonstrably resistant to change, a city that seemed to have laid out and reinforced a clear narrative about the Colonia and the people who lived there. This generation would experience many defeats, but there would also be some important victories, both personal and public.

In early April 1958, a story appeared in the "Young Americans" section of the *Oxnard Press-Courier* that got the whole town talking. According to the article, "Many Oxnard High School students are convinced that 'We absolutely have nothing now' in the way of a city recreation program for teenagers." In other words, there were too many teens hanging around with nothing to do.

So Oxnard officials decided it was time to build a new recreation center, putting aside an impressive $1 million for the project. To help the city get the biggest possible return on this investment, the local Soroptimist Club pitched in by conducting an anonymous survey of 2,300 Oxnard High School students to see what teens *really* wanted in a recreation center.

The results of the survey were disclosed in the "Young Americans" article.

Halls of Oxnard High School, 1962. *Courtesy of Bungalow Productions.*

A CERTAIN TIME FOR CERTAIN PEOPLE:
"YOU'RE GOING TO HAVE A RIOT ON YOUR HANDS"

According to the *Press-Courier*, most of the surveys gave answers detailing the kinds of programs and general atmosphere students sought. However, other answers revealed "some of the teenagers' own prejudices." The paper went on to quote some of the more incendiary responses it had received:

> *Said a junior girl: "Since my name is not being mentioned, I think the racial groups should be separated."*
>
> *Sophomore girl: "I think they should have certain nights for the different races."*
>
> *Freshman boy: "There should be a certain time for certain people to come to it."*
>
> *Junior boy: "The rec center should only allow quiet type teenagers and not the hoods or Pachucos or party breakers."*
>
> *Junior boy: "It be OK [sic] if they would keep the mexicans and whites separate. If you open a recreation center, there probably won't be very many*

kids going to it, because the decent people don't mix with the Mexicans. The mexicans huddle around in a corner trying to see how bad they are. When they start trying to push their luck, you're going to have a riot on your hands. In my opinion, there's no sense in building it because it will be over run by mexicans."

The article created such an uproar that one week later, a notice appeared in the newspaper that a "Prejudice Hearing" was to be held at the Juanita School auditorium in La Colonia. It announced, "An attempt to bring prejudice at Oxnard High School into the open will be made by the Oxnard Civic Improvement Association, according to its president A.T. Del Buono." The public was invited to attend.

Three hundred people, from both sides of the tracks, crowded into the auditorium on April 21. The following day's headline in the *Press-Courier* revealed the results of the conversation that ensued:

RACIAL DISCRIMINATION DENIED AT MEETING
The Press-Courier *was strongly criticized last night for publishing the story on the survey.*

"I feel that Mr. Kaminsky [Ralph Kaminsky, editor of the "Young Americans" page] *made an error in that particular article," said Mrs. Mary Harmon, president of the Soroptimist Club. She said that of the 2300 questionnaires filled out by students, only 12 gave any indications of favoring segregation.*

Dr. Joseph W. Crosby, superintendent of the high school district, commented: "We do not feel from the report of the survey that we have a serious problem at the school. We teach the students non-discrimination."

Many, it seemed, blamed the *Press-Courier*. "It caused tension at the school," said Tommie Board, a student at OHS, of the original article. "We should just drop the whole thing. Let's not talk about it. There's no discrimination at the school." Mrs. Mary Davis, then president-elect of the PTA, echoed the sentiment: "Oxnard High School has done a fine job….Parents should encourage their children to speak only English at home."

Others defended the newspaper. Mrs. Irene Mendoza, who had recently run for a spot on the school board, said, "I'm glad this came out in the paper. People will take better notice of things in Oxnard now."

The article, and the fallout, had clearly touched a nerve. In the years that followed, wildly differing points of view could be read in the *Press-Courier*—

not just in its articles but also in the editorial section—on the subject of prejudice in Oxnard. Some citizens flatly denied any inequities between the Colonia and the rest of Oxnard; others adamantly insisted that reform was long overdue.

POLICE QUELL PACHUCO RIOT: A MERRY CHASE

By the time they cropped up in the quotes from the teens in the "Young Americans" piece, terms like "Pachuco" (a word used to describe Mexican youths, usually derogatorily in association with gangs) and "riot" had appeared in the *Press-Courier* in relation to Colonia residents for several decades.

From October 28, 1940: "MOB ATTACKS LOCAL POLICE: OFFICERS CALLED TO QUELL MEXICAN RIOTS ON BOULEVARD."

From September 17, 1942: "AVERT MURDER BY TEAR GAS IN PACHUCO RIOT; KNIVES USED." The use of a tear gas bomb was reported on a Colonia crowd who was celebrating Mexican Independence Day when violent fighting began. A second tear gas bomb was later used to break up a fight. The number of citizens in attendance was not reported.

From October 4, 1944: "POLICE QUELL PACHUCO RIOT." "A wave of 'pachuco' madness has risen in Oxnard district again," the article opens, making a rhetorical link, though offering no evidence, between a "riot" comprising two cars containing Colonia boys (described as a "group of juvenile gangsters") who were being rowdy at the Fortuna Cafe on Oxnard Boulevard and an unrelated incident where a police officer had been hit in the head earlier in the week in another part of town. The article reports that the police gave the young men "a merry chase." Five were arrested.

From April 23, 1955: "POLICE QUELL COLONIA RIOT." "An angry milling mob of several hundred person [*sic*] cursed and spat upon Oxnard police officers in a riot in the Colonia area late last night following a fight among three teen-age youths," the newspaper reported.

Manuel Muñoz recalls this "riot" well. He was sixteen at the time.

It was just a misunderstanding....You could see if someone was out of place and didn't belong in our territory, shall we say. From out of town, like across the railroad tracks. I don't know....We survived and helped each other relax, blacks and Chicanos; I really don't know what side it was [who started the fighting], *but it was like a gang fight.*

Police Call for Help, Use Tear Gas To Quell 1,000-Man Colonia Riot

Sun & Tides—

Oxnard Press-Courier

Good Afternoon—

SERVING VENTURA COUNTY

OXNARD, CALIFORNIA, MONDAY, AUGUST 27, 1956

5 Men, 5 Teenagers Arrested In Rioting, Several Injured

By Don Schneider

Bulletin

Police Capture Suspects In Cafe Robbery Attempt

3 Men Jailed; Owner Gassed During Melee

5 Escape Death As Plane Clips Wire at Airport

2 Plead Innocent In $1 Million Hodge Conspiracy

Landslide Sends Picnickers Down 150-foot Cliff

Tennessee Pupils Picket First School Integration

1 Killed, 200 Hurt In Riots in India

Japanese Didn't Spot Russian H-Bomb Test

WHEN I SAY "JUMP"-JUMP

INDEX

3 Sailors Killed; 4 Injured in Crash

Front page of the *Oxnard Press-Courier*, August 27, 1956. The photos are unrelated to the article reporting the riot, in which ten were arrested. *Image from* Oxnard Press-Courier.

Things got bigger and bigger, so people started getting meaner and meaner and started throwing things around, and before I knew it, it got out of hand. Our police officials…there were not so many in those days on the police force.

It's of course impossible to know for certain the effect of this type of reporting on the general public's perception of the Colonia. But by 1958, according to the *Press-Courier*, at least one student at Oxnard High School was under the impression that any gathering of his fellow students who happened to be of Mexican descent would lead to a riot.

Cesar Returns:
"I Just Wanted to Go Back and Fight"

The Community Service Organization, or CSO, was founded in the late 1940s by veteran organizers Fred Ross, Antonio Rios and Edward Roybal, who would go on to serve in the U.S. Congress, founding the Congressional Hispanic Caucus. The CSO has become known to history for training both Cesar Chavez and Dolores Huerta in activism.

In 1958, when its national leaders agreed the time was right to send someone to help the local chapter in Oxnard, the CSO decided to send Cesar Chavez. Because of his traumatic childhood experiences of poverty in La Colonia, Chavez explained in *Cesar Chavez: Autobiography of La Causa*, returning to Oxnard was not an easy decision:

When we were migrants, Oxnard was an extremely bad place for us. In the back of my mind I thought that going back would be a little revenge. I just wanted to go back and fight.

…The first thing I did was to start house meetings. Then we started a voter registration drive, because the November election was coming up and there was a good Democrat running there.…I began to sign up people for citizenship classes and opened a little office about the third day I was there to service the people.

So in the same year the article about the recreation center appeared in the *Press-Courier*, when hundreds of citizens had gathered to debate whether prejudice existed among the city's youth, Cesar returned. This time he was not in the Colonia to pick walnuts. This time he was not a child heading off

Cesar Chavez prepares to speak in Oxnard, 1970. *Image from* Oxnard Press-Courier.

to school without shoes. But he was there to help those who were, and this time he had backup.

On November 1, 1958, his arrival was announced without fanfare in a small item that appeared on page 8 of the *Press-Courier*:

> CSO OPENS DRIVE TO GET OUT VOTE
> *The Community Service Organization is promoting a drive to get out the vote in Oxnard.*
>
> *In charge of the campaign are Cesar Chavez, national organizational director for Community Service Organizations, and John Soria of the local CSO.*
>
> *The vote drive will be strictly non-partisan, Mr. Soria said. The purpose of it is to overcome public apathy and get people to the poll.*
>
> *The group will have a large number of volunteers at all precincts to provide phone service and transportation. Headquarters of the group is at 435 North Hayes avenue.*

The article made no mention of Cesar's personal history with La Colonia; in fact, it would go virtually unreported in Oxnard during his lifetime. But the other gentleman mentioned in the short piece, "John" Soria, was a legendary figure who was *very* familiar to Oxnard readers, even in 1958.

BIG JUAN: HE WAS LIKE A GENTLE GIANT

In 1950, the *Press-Courier* published a feature on a star athlete from Oxnard High School. The paper frequently lauded local youth who had achieved on the gridiron, diamond or court. But this feature was a bit different. For one thing, as the paper noted, at six foot five and approximately three hundred pounds, the boy was much, much larger than the average high school student, and for another, he was Mexican American. Nevertheless, the *Press-Courier* extolled the boy's talents, stating, "Not only is John Soria just about the biggest athlete to ever to wear the colors of Oxnard High, he is also developing into one of the best."

Juan Soria (or "Big John," as he'd been dubbed by then) was larger than life. But even the biggest figures in history start out small. Born and raised in La Colonia by parents who spoke little English, Juan's first day of elementary school did not go well. His wife, Catalina Soria, describes the painful and formative events that unfolded:

> When Juan first went to school he couldn't speak English well. He wanted to use the restroom and he kept asking, but in Spanish. So, he said, the teacher tied him to the flagpole. They tied him to the American flag, so Juan could learn it was important to speak English. Of course, he wet his pants. Can you imagine what a brutal experience that was? No wonder he became such a rebel.

But by 1950, when the *Press-Courier* praised his athleticism, Juan was well known to the people behind the paper. In fact, he was working there himself as a printer's devil (an apprenticeship-type position), and five years earlier, he'd had a job as a paperboy.

Being a paperboy in La Colonia in the mid-1940s was a very dangerous business. Though the rest of Oxnard had had paved roads and expansive sidewalks for decades, Colonia streets were unpaved and there were no sidewalks. Shortly before Soria got his own route, a paperboy from the barrio had been killed by a car. But it was a job Soria badly needed because, as the *Press-Courier* reported in 1945, he'd been recently orphaned.

There's no good way to become an orphan. Soria's father was from Nayarit and his mother from Michoacán. Not too long after arriving in Oxnard, they opened the Fortuna Café, the eatery mentioned in the "Pachuco Madness" article of 1944. When Juan was thirteen, both his parents died in a murder-suicide. The newspaper described how Juan

Juan Soria, from an unsuccessful run for Oxnard City Council, 1960. *Image from* Oxnard Press-Courier.

and his five siblings were struggling to stay together and keep the business afloat. After several weeks, readers learned, the siblings had been taken in by Colonia neighbors in two separate households. The effects of the restaurant were sold to help pay for their upkeep. It was a cataclysmic event in an already challenging life.

Despite his publicly rocky start, by high school, Juan Soria's athletic achievements had made him a household name. After graduation, he became the first member of his family to attend college, first at Midwestern University and then back in Ventura County.

When Juan returned to his hometown, he was welcomed warmly. Oxnard couldn't wait for him to lend his talents to the Ventura team. But there was a problem. Midwestern wouldn't release his transcripts, claiming he owed $110 for transportation—money the student did not have and could not earn in time. Once again, Soria's name appeared in the newspaper, this time in an appeal for the town to chip in and help secure his academic future—not to mention his athletic one. In October 1952, an editorial in the *Press-Courier* heralded the results: "A number of the Latin-American groups in the city have made up a fund of $110 for John Soria, which will clear his standing with Midwestern University, and open up the possibility of his playing football at Ventura College where he is now enrolled."

Soria's youngest daughter, Isabel Soria, was unaware of the community's efforts to help her father, who would go on to return the favor many times over. Upon learning of this event, she became quite emotional and shared a bit about her father's character.

I don't know why that affected me. I'm sorry! If you knew my dad, he was so proud. And I think it was overcompensating, you know, for being an orphan. He was humble and very much about the people. He was like a gentle giant. He usually kept his composure. He cared about people, so much more than himself.

Juan Soria attempts to fight voter suppression of elderly Colonia residents, 1960. *Image from Oxnard Press-Courier.*

From his early childhood in his parents' restaurant until his final days in Oxnard, Juan Soria never stopped working. While in college in Ventura, he also worked at the American Crystal Sugar Company as a warehouseman. After he'd graduated and started a family with his first wife, Julieta, Soria was doing everything he could to help the people of Oxnard—especially his neighbors in the Colonia.

He started at the CSO in 1958. It was there that he first met Cesar Chavez. They formed a long working relationship that lasted for many years, during which Chavez would return to La Colonia again and again. Catalina Soria reflects on the respect Soria had for Chavez:

> Bueno, *Cesar Chavez, he had charisma. Some people just have that kind of magnetism that you just listen to them. He had it….Like one time, Chavez said,* "A los puercos también los oyes hacer ruido cuando

están tragando" *(even pigs make noise when they are swallowing)* or *something to that effect. Juan would explain to me about Cesar, "He's achieving.* Tiene magnetismo.*!"*

Throughout the 1960s, Juan Soria was involved with many organizations in his countless efforts to improve life for Oxnard's workers. After the CSO, he served as director of the Oxnard Farm Workers Service Center and worked statewide with the United Packinghouse Workers, the United Brotherhood of Teamsters and the Emergency Committee to Aid Farmworkers. The movement faced an uphill battle throughout the state of California. Catalina Soria looks back on its effect on Oxnard: "The movement in Oxnard, it was okay. Because the biggest source of income there was agriculture. So when [organizers] tried to encourage the *huelga* [strike], they got mobility! It could have been worse."

Juan Soria was relentless in his mission to advance civil rights in Oxnard. But the *Press-Courier*, which had loved him when he was scoring points on the football field, did not take such a favorable view of his activism. In 1965, Soria and Anthony Del Buono (the civic leader who had organized the open meeting to discuss prejudice at Oxnard High School) teamed up to protest the local Elks Club. An editorial mocked their concern:

> *Now a meeting at the Oxnard Elks Club was to be picketed on the grounds that the Elks do not admit Negroes to membership. The two men who say this is pretty awful are Tony Del Buono and John Soria.*
>
> *Since Soria grew up in Oxnard, it is most unlikely that he has suddenly discovered this problem that so offends him. Del Buono also has been in the county long enough to be reasonably well informed. But the shock of realization has overwhelmed them, and they cannot wait to take the first opportunity to register their protest.*

Juan Soria's activism, and his many runs for office, did not come without a personal price tag. His first marriage faltered, and his bank account wasn't what it might have been if he'd lent his formidable intelligence and resourcefulness to a more profitable vocation. As his daughter recalls:

> *Sometimes I think he wasn't able to accomplish everything he wanted to accomplish. Dad was not motivated by financial gain. So I admire him, I admire so much that he wanted to help people his whole life. But who was helping* him, *you know?*

Yeah, "Big John" Soria. Whenever he would run for office, he would always use the name Juan and they would turn around and call him "Big John Soria." He never had enough money to really run for office. But Dad would always turn out the Latino vote.

The *Press-Courier*'s reports of Soria's career in politics and activism grew increasingly dismissive throughout the 1960s. But in 1970, Soria made a move that caught many in its readership completely off guard. It would effect a massive shift that has changed the trajectory of an ever-growing number of lives in Oxnard: *Soria v. Oxnard School Board of Trustees.* Juan Soria was putting his considerable strength into ending segregation and inequity in Oxnard once and for all, in perhaps the only place it could ever really be done: the schools.

By the end of the 1960s, the State of California was putting pressure on the City of Oxnard to end the de facto segregation that had been caused by years of geographic and legislative isolation of the Colonia. The city could not agree about the best way to desegregate the schools to the satisfaction of the state, causing serious delays. Many were resistant to the idea of integration altogether. In 1969, just months before Juan Soria filed his case, the newspaper recorded a meeting of the school board:

Tuesday night's discussion opened with a report by Asst. Supt. Dr. Gregory Betts on four studies completed last spring regarding the educational progress of Colonia youngsters.

These indicated generally that Colonia children educated in racially balanced schools did better than those whose instruction had been in schools with de facto segregation.

Acting Supt. S.H. Stewart, said that while not "statistically unassailable," the studies seem to confirm the superiority of integrated to segregated education.

...In separate action the board rejected on a 3–2 vote a resolution of [Trustee] *Tinklepaugh requesting the state to pay for greatly-expanded special programs in the district aimed at the culturally deprived child.*

Tinklepaugh explained that he felt the state had "pretty well forced a program on us," and he thought the state should pay for it.

The public was also greatly conflicted, and the debate waged on in the *Press-Courier* for months. On April 30, 1969, in a letter to the editor, Henry J. Johnson declared:

Until 1954, both Colonia schools held "double-session" days in an attempt to manage overcrowding rather than busing children to less crowded schools outside the Colonia. *Image from* Oxnard Press-Courier.

It is doubtful that America's Negro and Mexican-American populations have an average intelligence quotient (I.Q.) equal to that of the average white American family. There are many reasons for this, mainly that the minority elements represent their own homelands' lower, or peasant, classes rather than the more intelligent levels.

This opinion was immediately countered by another letter to the editor the following week from three citizens: Elaine Cooluris, Gerhard Orthuber and Lino Corona:

We…feel it very unconvincing of some people to express shock by the recent uncovery of the ethnic imbalance which exists in the Oxnard elementary schools.…Segregation has existed in Oxnard a great many years. These "unaware" people know exactly what percent of their tax dollars are spent on education, exactly how much interest they pay on their cars, exactly when their insurance premiums are due, and yet, when it comes to something as apparent as segregation they develop an incurable case of blindness. It is easy to feign blindness if one does not wish to see.

Soria v. Oxnard School Board of Trustees was filed on February 20, 1970. In Dr. David G. Garcia's book *Strategies of Segregation*, he outlines the approach of the ultimately successful case:

Working out of an office on Cooper Road in La Colonia, attorney Gerhard W. Orthuber [who had penned the response to Mr. Johnson in the *Press-Courier*] *and community organizer Juan L. Soria collaboratively developed a legal complaint that attempted to simultaneously challenge de facto and de jure segregation—charging the trustees of knowingly maintaining and purposefully perpetuating segregated schooling.*

Soria and the rest of the team put together a very compelling case, and they won. It was a major turning point for Oxnard; it was also a personal turning point for Soria. Catalina Soria remembers it well. The groundbreaking case brought her and Juan together. She'd recently started working at the Legal Aid office in Colonia.

Fred Olson, my boss, was white, as was just about every attorney. All the assistants were minorities. Well, we had to be, in order to be bilingual. At Legal Aid, it was all domestic cases, no criminal law.

I met Juan because he was bringing Fred Olson into a civil matter for the school district case. Juan came into Legal Aid and asked if I was Mrs. Frazier [her first husband was deceased]. I said, "Yes, I am." So he pulled up a chair, and we started talking about the landmark case. I'd recently put my son in public school in Oxnard. I said to Juan, "I'll be a plaintiff."

Catalina was already a vocal supporter of the activism that was going on at the time, but she noticed that sometimes Juan met resistance from the very people they were trying to help.

He would say, "Tienes que enseñarles que su pan tiene mantequilla. Porque tú tienes la razón. *(You have to show them their bread and butter is at stake. Because you are in the right.) You have to sell your values with logic!" He used to use so many* dichos *(Mexican proverbs). I love them. Some looked at Juan as an "uppity Mexican" and would try to put him down, but I looked up to him tremendously.*

After the case was won in May 1971, the city finally took concerted action to create equity in its schools. Juan Soria continued to fight for the community that had in many ways become his family, making an impact on other big issues like affordable housing. People often say Juan "cast a big shadow," but that sometimes made it easy to miss the toll his life of service was taking on his health and relationships. Back when he was winning trophies for OHS and Ventura College, no one wondered why "Big John" was so big. While many Colonia adults reportedly turned to alcohol to deal with the relentless pressure, Juan Soria took a slightly different path in order to cope. His daughter Isabel explains:

He did all these things that he struggled for, and I think especially how it was an uphill battle.…So many people that are old-timers now, they couldn't live wherever they wanted. They couldn't buy property wherever they wanted or even vote. People were doing backbreaking work and not moving forward.

It shaped who my dad was. I always think about that; if his parents hadn't died when he was thirteen, maybe he would have been different. But still, he was a product of his environment, of his community. There was only so much they allowed Mexicans to do. My dad actually did not drink at all. He smoked cigarettes, like so many did in his time, and he overate… diabetes and so on. He ended up being a double amputee because of it.

His wife, too, experienced frustration that the man who always dropped everything to go the extra mile for others, even strangers, was sometimes unwilling to take care of himself. At age sixty-five, seemingly indomitable and still larger than life, Juan Soria died of a heart attack. Catalina recalls:

> *When he died, the next school that was to be built was supposed to be named Juan Soria School....Instead, when the next school was built, they named it after Norman Brekke* [former superintendent who had opposed the Soria case]. *Then, the next school was supposed to be named after Juan, but right before they built it, Thurgood Marshall had died.*

The family and the community began to think that Soria would never get the recognition he deserved. Isabel Soria recalls, "Quite a bit of time had passed since my dad died, so I was thinking, 'Oh, they're not going to build the school.' I thought they wouldn't because so many of his friends had died by then, too."

But then in 2009, a dozen years after Soria's passing, the city finally opened a state-of-the-art facility in his name. It had been a long time coming.

Juan Soria School, Oxnard, 2018. *Photo by author.*

A school. A place where children would be given opportunities that had never been afforded to Juan Soria. It may be difficult to understand why he persisted as he did against seemingly insurmountable odds, but those who knew him best agree: he simply loved Oxnard.

> *One time, my dad was driving us to Rose Park. He was taking us there by going through the Colonia. I asked him, "Why are we taking this way, Dad?" He said, "I want to show you something." Then he gestured around the Colonia and said, "This is a beautiful area. Oxnard is beautiful. Everyone loves the weather here. You can grow anything here." I think I'd asked him how come he'd never left Oxnard. As he drove through Colonia, he said, "Look at these flowers. You're not going to get these flowers in other cities. This is the Colonia; look how beautiful." And he's showing me these different gardens, and everyone's got their corn and their beautiful flowers. And now that I've moved away, I think, "I miss Oxnard. I miss the beautiful weather. It's beautiful. You can grow anything there." He loved Oxnard. He just loved it.*

BEANY HATS OR BROWN BERETS?: VAST POTENTIAL FOR BETTERING CONDITIONS

While Juan Soria and Cesar Chavez were busy organizing in labor and education, the youth of the Colonia was also getting involved not just in these local issues but in national ones as well. Lupe Lujan recalls:

> *My sister and I got exposed to some of the political matters because we were teaching English to migrant farmworkers through Juan Soria. He hired us, and we were teaching ESL in the little building that's still there on Colonia Road. I became more aware of what was happening through that job because we had to go to conferences. There were some marches in Colonia and downtown during the Vietnam War by the students and the Brown Berets.*

Ofelia Rodriguez, who, like Lupe, was part of the first generation of Colonia kids to attend college, remembers those heady times:

> *I was in the Brown Berets. My first husband was one of the ones who founded the chapter. We were all in it....I also worked with the Quakers;*

they came in and set up an office in Colonia near the tracks. The Friends. They did research and took pictures of the campesinos' *conditions, their work conditions, and they produced these reports that had pictures of how they had no toilet facilities and no drinking water.*

The Brown Berets had chapters springing up all over the Southwest in the late 1960s. Dr. Isidro Ortiz, professor of Chicano studies at San Diego State University, offers some insight on how groups like the Berets evolved:

In the late 1960s…some students formed civic organizations to be more visible in the community, to interact with each other and build solidarity. Some had gone on to form an organization, the Brown Berets. A more militant organization but nevertheless one that reflected the rising solidarity and the unity among youth in this period. Organizations such as this helped develop a sense of self-efficacy—an idea that, if they acted, they could indeed make a difference.

The Oxnard chapter was founded by Colonia natives who had returned to the barrio from college and were determined to improve conditions there. According to the *Press-Courier*, they didn't quite get off on the right foot.

The Berets first came to the public's attention in 1968, when the newspaper reported on a flyer they had distributed. In it, according to the paper, the group had "referred to Oxnard Police officers as 'white racist cops,' 'helmeted goons' and 'white helmeted dogs.'" As a result, public perception of the Brown Berets in Oxnard was a mixed bag, to say the least. Many viewed them with suspicion. Even Colonia residents were not sure how they felt about what one Colonia man called "the self-proclaimed 'beany hats,' Brown Berets."

Shortly after the flyer kerfuffle, a *Press-Courier* journalist named Bea Hartmann published a series of articles to help readers understand what the young activists were actually trying to achieve.

The Brown Berets, who are admittedly "aggressive in spirit," [are] headquartered at 130 Colonia Road—the address of the American Friends Service Committee, a branch of the Religious Society of Friends (Quakers). The personable young men leading the all Mexican-American organization cry out for a better life and a better understanding of their people.

…Each official within the organization, it appears, has his own idea of which is the major problem in the area. With Armando Lopez it is

Former site of Neighborhood Youth Corps, Oxnard, 2018. *Photo by author.*

inadequate housing. With Roberto Flores it is education. With Andres Herrera it appears to be lack of citizen awareness in general.

Hartmann then proceeded to break down, issue by issue, the main concerns of the Berets and their ideas for improving life in the Colonia. She concludes, "It appears the Brown Berets have a vast potential for bettering conditions for the Mexican-American population of Oxnard if they are wisely led and diligently working toward that purpose."

Dr. Ortiz describes the lasting impact of groups like the Brown Berets:

> *They legitimated a form of action that continues into the present and that, I think, will remain the main form of political activism for students in schools given that, for many young people, the vote has not been a mechanism by which they could affect change. That certainly was the case in 1968 when,* *of course, if you were under 21 you could not vote* [in most states]. *So young people turned to that form of politics, the strategy of the powerless: protest. Protest has been one of the major traditions in American history.*

The fight for progress and justice in La Colonia occurred on many fronts. It had its heroes and villains and even some unlikely allies.

FLASHPOINT: "IF YOU GET ARRESTED, I'M NOT BAILING YOU OUT"

Bruce Smith was a college student when he first became aware of the political and social maelstrom that was swirling around the Colonia. He'd traveled through Oxnard to participate in the Vietnam War protests that had engulfed the city of Santa Barbara, just north of Oxnard, and had erupted into the infamous Isla Vista riots of 1970.

> *Well, it was the age where many of my fellow students were heavily engaged in politics. A lot of it was about racial prejudice and profiling and the unjustness of all of that, and then it became much broader in the context of the Vietnam War. And that became a flashpoint. It was part of the mix, it was a call to our generation to be much more politically involved than our parents.*
>
> *My mother was supportive. She always asked a lot of questions to try and get me to think about the ramifications of my actions. My father basically said, "Well, if you get arrested, I'm not bailing you out."*

Isla Vista Bank of America burns down in riot, 1970. *Image from* Oxnard Press-Courier.

After college, Smith went to work for the City of Oxnard as an urban planner, a job in which he became acquainted with the Colonia and the problems of its residents. From there, Smith got a job with Ventura County. But by then he was also deeply involved with another line of work: helping organize the farm and factory workers of Ventura County, including in Oxnard. His colleagues at the county were unaware of his activities, and he was able to maintain something of a double life for some time.

> *I was careful to keep my identity as a city or state employee separate from my free speech rights. So I didn't make it a point of going up and telling anybody, "Oh, guess where I work?" I probably would have been asked to cease and desist....So I kept them separate.*
>
> *Then the next major visit I had in the Colonia was when I became involved with a farmworkers' advocacy group that was centered out of UCSB, and their gift to that cause was to perform street theater, or street acting, to make people aware of the plight of farmworkers. The play was mainly little set-ups here and there. We would alter it for the local audience with little snippets of interactions and we would mix and match them, depending on who the audience was.*
>
> *The first time we went out together, it was to Julius Goldman's Egg City, out in Moorpark in the mid-1970s. There was a labor strike going on, and so our group performed for the farmworkers and the protestors....After that I think there was another case of successful unionizing of farmworkers in Ventura County. It was then that some things started happening.*

Street theater of the kind Smith participated in, like the Delano-based "Teatro Campesino," was a powerful force in the labor movement in the 1960s and 1970s. By presenting characters audiences could relate to in situations they themselves were grappling with, street theater helped organize and empower an underserved populace to express their needs. Though Smith usually worked offstage, he recalls being asked to improvise for a performance in La Colonia:

> *I was asked to go an event in Rose Park in La Colonia. It was sort of a last-minute thing. When we got there the actors said, "Oh hey, by the way, the guy who usually plays the part of the* la migra [immigration] *representative can't make it. Do you mind taking his part?" Having done some community theater before, I said, "Well, I'm not afraid of getting on a stage or projecting voice, but I don't speak Spanish!" And they said, "Perfect!"*

…We were asked to do our skit onstage, and it was pretty well received. I was really surprised by the guffaws that I received when I delivered my lines! I guess I was doing an amazing job at really doing a number on the language. And then immediately after, while we were still onstage, Cesar Chavez stepped onto the stage with us.

Smith was unaware that Chavez would be speaking at the event. There had been rumors, but most had expected that a surrogate would be sent in Chavez's place.

Above: Cesar Chavez addresses a Colonia crowd at one of many visits to the barrio, 1974. *Image from* Oxnard Press-Courier.

Left: The Muñoz family, Oxnard, 1960s. *Courtesy of Martha Muñoz Rodriguez.*

A lot of it was encouraging mutual support, especially Hispanic to Hispanic, that "we don't have to take this." Because a lot of farmworkers were, as they are today, afraid of raising their head because of fear of deportation or just simply because they didn't know [the workings of] *the system or the English language. It was encouraging them that together, in a collective bond, they were stronger than they would be individually.*

For those born in the Colonia during the 1930s and 1940s, the city of Oxnard was full of people who had already made up their minds about them. There were systems in place to keep them from expanding beyond the boundaries of the neighborhood in every sense. And yet, there was always a steadfast spirit that endured in spite of it all. People in La Colonia are very fond of *dichos*, old proverbs passed down through generations. A favorite *dicho*, adapted from a Greek saying and made popular during the Mexican revolution, is "*Quisieron enterrarnos, pero no sabían que éramos semillas.*" [They tried to bury us, but they didn't know we were seeds.]

CHAPTER 6

ROBERTO

"Due in La Colonia"

O n May 27, 1968, the *Oxnard Press-Courier* announced an event that Colonia residents would never forget:

> *Sen. Robert F. Kennedy's presidential bandwagon will roar through Ventura County late Tuesday, when the candidate will motor*[cade] *on a handshaking ride from Oxnard's Colonia to the airport....*
>
> *"We're encouraging Colonia and downtown residents to be on the motor route," Kennedy's aide said. "People from Port Hueneme and the beach areas are encouraged to go to the airport."*
>
> *A report that California farm labor leader Cesar Chavez would be in Oxnard to greet Kennedy could not be confirmed.*

Kennedy had long been a supporter of the farmworkers and Cesar Chavez, but no one expected him to stop in Oxnard, let alone visit the tiny barrio of La Colonia. The campaign stop had been organized locally, in large part by Juan Soria. Though the senator's visit occurred before they were married, Soria's second wife, Catalina, recalls it clearly: "Robert Kennedy was running for president. Juan organized his campaign. My son remembers it well, that the motorcade went right by our house. Juan and I hadn't met yet!"

Manuel Muñoz will never forget that day either:

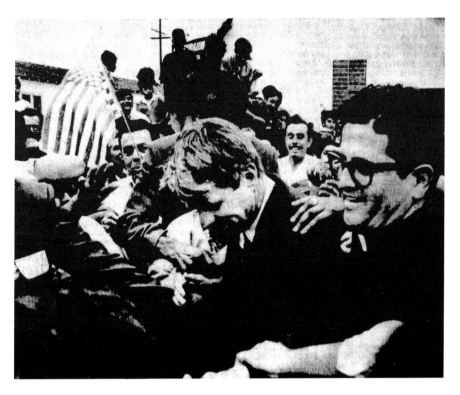

Senator Robert F. Kennedy, *left*, shakes hands with Colonia residents alongside Colonia priest Father Madera, May 28, 1968. *Image from* Oxnard Press-Courier.

I think my most amazing memory of anything that ever happened in Colonia was when Robert Kennedy came. He was standing up in a convertible. And Rafer Johnson, the Olympic champion, was holding his legs so he wouldn't fall off.

They drove by real fast down First, then to Juanita, to Cooper and then to the church. Father Madera, he's the one that greeted him at the church. He went in with him and they went way up to the front and prayed. I didn't make it that far because they were going too fast. It was exciting. He was running for president! He was quite a sight for sore eyes for practically the whole city. Especially since he went through the Colonia; that was pretty amazing. That's about all I can tell you about it. I'll tell you the honest truth, I'm seventy-nine, and memories like that? They're what keep me alive.

Muñoz's youngest sister, Martha Muñoz Rodriguez, also remembers the visit. She had made it to the small cinder block church of Cristo Rey that

Senator Robert F. Kennedy, *center*, kneels in prayer at the altar of the Colonia church of Cristo Rey, Oxnard, May 28, 1968. *Image from* Oxnard Press-Courier.

day. "When Bobby Kennedy came, he was at the church. I just stood in the corner. I couldn't get very close. I saw the motorcade."

"Roberto" had come to mean a great deal to Mexican Americans across the country, and for the people of La Colonia, he inspired hope for a brighter future. Just eight days later, Robert F. Kennedy was dead. Olympic medalist Rafer Johnson, who had kept the senator from falling out of the convertible when his motorcade passed through La Colonia, was one of three men, along with football player Rosey Grier and journalist George Plimpton, who tackled Sirhan Sirhan immediately following the assassination.

HEY LULU, THEY KILLED ROBERT KENNEDY, *POBRECITO*

As shockwaves of the event reached the Colonia, the entire community *se pusieron de luto* (went into mourning). Joe and Rachel Anguiano were worried. Joe's sister Lupe had been in Ambassador Hotel that night. Rachel remembers:

> *Lupe worked for Cesar Chavez. She organized a grape strike in Michigan and Ohio with him. Lupe was a nun, and she got out of the nunhood…and*

she campaigned for Robert Kennedy. And she was there when he got shot. So she and Dolores Huerta came to our house that following day. They were just in shock. I remember I was ironing and I heard a knock at the door, and it was Lupe and her friend.

The *Press-Courier* recorded the reaction of La Colonia to the news:

Bells pealed early today in Oxnard's Colonia, and their dying sound will linger in the community for years to come. The Colonia; where Mexican-Americans almost to a person went to the polls Tuesday to cast their lot with the man who now lies dead. Nine days ago Robert Kennedy had chosen to be amongst them.

Today…where Kennedy had kneeled before the altar, Father Jose Madera stood at 7:30 this morning, hands extended to Providence, offering a special mass. Old women knelt in the pews, wearing dark veils, and among them was a newsboy and a girl with a sheer white veil over long blond hair.

Tapestries on the wall told the "Way of the Cross." Robert Kennedy had been here before.

Only once did Father Madera, as he said the Mass, seem to shy from the now painful memories before him.

Before breaking the Host, he lifted his eyeglasses ever so slightly. "Roberto," he said softly, then seemed to wipe away a tear.

"Some of the people are saying there's no reason to vote now," said Father Jose Madera, assistant pastor at Christ the King Catholic church in Oxnard's Colonia.

The assassination of Sen. Robert F. Kennedy smote hard the hopes of the Mexican-Americans and Negroes in Colonia. He was their champion.

It was their confidance [sic] in Sen. Kennedy's espousal of the cause of the impoverished, nurtured by fond memories of his brother, the late President, that brought Colonia residents to the polls Tuesday in large numbers to vote for him 10–1 over Sen. Eugene McCarthy.

…"No one knows what leader will arise now," said Father Madera. "Some of the people say it's no use to vote-in a leader because someone will shoot him," he said.

Robert Kennedy, during an interlude in his recent campaign through Ventura County, stopped in Christ the King Church and mentioned to Father Madera his pleasure at the "goodwill of the people here…he said he was pleased that they were so spontaneous," the priest said.

Memorial Mass for Robert F. Kennedy, Colonia church of Cristo Rey, Oxnard, June 1968. *Image from* Oxnard Press-Courier.

He told Father Madera that he was "happy in his campaign" but somewhat fatigued.

"Offered refreshment, he declined saying that he just wanted to pray a little…to make a visit to the Blessed Sacrament."

He prayed. He made his visit. He left the church to the cries of "Viva Kennedy" (Long live Kennedy).

Juan Soria, who had helped orchestrate the campaign stop in Oxnard, was inconsolable. His wife recalls that dark time:

Then Kennedy got killed. I remember I'd gone to bed early that night because I didn't want to stay up late and see the results [of the primary]. *I went to work the next day, and they said, "They killed Kennedy." I remember I went to the church; it was next door to Legal Aid, where I worked.*

Juan told me later, even though he wasn't a drinker, he went and got so drunk. He said he drank and cried for three days straight. I have beautiful letters from Lyndon Johnson to Juan, thanking him for his work on the campaign, and from Reies Tijerina [major figure of the Chicano movement who fought to restore land grants in New Mexico to their original owners] *calling Juan* "hermano de la lucha" [brother in the struggle].

Manuel Muñoz, too, was shocked. Just eight days earlier, he'd seen Kennedy with his own eyes in his own barrio: "Not too long after that was when he was assassinated, at that hotel in LA. I told my sister, 'Hey Lulu, they killed Robert Kennedy, *pobrecito.*'"

HIS MEMORY LINGERS ON

The loss of such an important national figure who had stopped to personally touch the people of the Colonia was deep. Even now, those who were there the day he drove by *their* homes and stores, shaking hands before praying in *their* church, hold the memory very close to the surface.

In the days that followed, the *Press-Courier* described how the barrio continued to mark the loss. A collection was made among Colonia neighbors, amassing seventy-five dollars, to send flowers to Kennedy's final resting place in Arlington Cemetery. For many, it was money they could ill afford to part with. But in the Colonia, that's what you do for family.

On June 9, the *Press-Courier* reported, the barrio filled the streets again in silent procession.

> *Thousands of Colonia residents and many from surrounding areas joined citizens from throughout the nation Sunday in attending religious services in memory of the late Sen. Robert F. Kennedy, slain by an assassin's bullet last Wednesday. The Rev. J.J. Arredondo, pastor of the Christ the King Church and the Rev. Jose de Jesus Madera, assistant pastor, led a silent procession that began at the church on Cooper Road, then moved east to Juanita Avenue ending at Our Lady of Guadalupe School grounds.*
>
> *At the school, an evening mass was celebrated followed by eulogies.... "The passing of this man is tragic, nothing will change it, but his memory lingers on, for no one man is alone in his beliefs, his goals or his aspirations, May God rest his soul in peace and give us strength in our quest for securing peace, and making this a better world to live in for all," Father Madera concluded.*
>
> *During the services many, both men and women, wiped tears from their eyes as they sat with their heads bowed in prayer—each remembering the senator's visit to the city last May 28.*

Silent procession for Robert F. Kennedy, Colonia, Oxnard, June 1968. *Image from* Oxnard Press-Courier.

CHAPTER **7**

THE CHURCHES

The fourth installment of Don W. Martin's "Colonia" series introduced *Press-Courier* readers to perhaps the most well-known figure in the barrio.

THEY'RE GOOD KIDS

We have said that Colonia has a relatively low crime rate, among juveniles as well as adults.

On the juvenile aspect, a good part of the credit must go to one man— Father Madera.

…Father Madera is one of three priests at Christ the King Catholic Church.…His particular dedication is to youth.

When [he] came to Colonia three years ago…there was little organized youth activity.…Too frequently, teenage activity was the kind that made the police blotter.

The priest was already renowned for his ability to connect with neighborhood youth. By 1963, when this article was published, Cristo Rey parish had gone from one group with eighteen members to six groups totaling over one hundred teens among its ranks.

[Madera] *held up a recent copy of the* Press-Courier, *which bannered the story of two youths killed, in an auto crash recently. Both were from Colonia. "My youngsters raised money for the families of these boys," he said. "And more than 80 attended a mass for them. They're good kids."*

…The father's largest group is the Catholic Youth Organization, which numbers 65 teenage boys and girls. Locally, they're known as the "Roman Imperials." The father frowned. "But they have picked a very poor nickname for themselves. They call themselves the 'Playboys' and 'PlayGirls.'

"I don't think they realize the true significance of these foolish names," he said.

Father Joe Madera leads teenagers in a Colonia Park workout, Oxnard, 1963. *Image from* Oxnard Press-Courier.

Oxnard is still overwhelmingly Catholic; this group makes up the largest demographic block among religious residents. Many Colonia natives report having felt excluded in the past from Oxnard's largest Catholic church, Santa Clara, and expressed a preference for attending the barrio churches.

Not a single interview conducted for this book failed to mention the positive impact the Colonia churches and priests had in people's lives. Most mentioned, by name, either Father Joe Madera or Father John Fosselman, the priest into whose parish Madera had transferred from Los Angeles.

ALTAR BOY

Bob Herrera, who worshiped in the Colonia churches long before the arrival of Father Joe, has fond memories of him and Father John:

I used to be an altar boy at the Santa Clarita chapel, my brother Ben and myself. It was Father John; he was a German priest. Very young…he was very famous.

110

We went to Our Lady of Guadalupe on Meta Street. They built another church before, on Grant [the Chapel of St. John Vianney]. *I remember from way back, maybe 1940. It was the little church, they moved it. They actually picked it up and moved it to Cooper Road.* Dónde está Christ the King Church. *It was a wooden structure; it's still there. But it was originally on Grant.*

Mira que Father Madera, que estaba bien conocido. [Look at Father Madera, he became very well known.] *Then there was Robert Kennedy; he knew him. He was such a wonderful priest.*

A MODERN ADOBE

In 1954, the *Press-Courier* announced the building of a new elementary school at Christ the King church. The church itself was new to the barrio, and like the later churches of Our Lady of Guadalupe, St. Anthony and the remodeled Santa Clarita Chapel (the oldest in the area), it was overseen by Monsignor Jacobs of Santa Clara Church.

Exterior of Christ the King church, also known as Cristo Rey, La Colonia, Oxnard, 2018. *Photo by author.*

[The church] *serves the Spanish-speaking people and is known by them as Cristo Rey....Built entirely of rocklite blocks, which resembles a modern adobe appearance, the building was designed by the Right Reverend Monsignor Anthony J. Jacobs, pastor of the Santa Clara Church. It was constructed in 1951 at a cost of $80,000.*

While everyone interviewed mentioned that they'd worshiped at at least one of the Colonia churches, only a few mentioned experiences at Santa Clara, home to Monsignor Jacobs.

WE REALLY STICK OUT

Corinne Estrada did her early sacraments at Santa Clara since she and her brother were enrolled in the elementary school there: "When we made our First Holy Communion, everyone was in white and we were all up on stage on risers so you could see each child. There were only a few of us Mexican kids. You didn't have to work too hard to find us. I thought, 'Oh my, we really stick out.'"

Exterior of Santa Clara Church, Oxnard, 2018. *Courtesy of Lupe Lujan.*

Big Jake

Ofelia Rodriguez remembers that Monsignor Jacobs had a nickname in the Colonia: "Big Jake."

> *Nowadays, Cristo Rey is only used once in a while. Like for a funeral, if Guadalupe is not available. I once heard something, I don't know if it's true, but…well, Christ the King has never been a beautiful church, it's cinder block, and Santa Clara is such a beautiful church, right?*
>
> *I remember there was a rumor about "Big Jake" from Santa Clara, which was what they called Monsignor Jacobs years ago.…The rumor was that he did not want Christ the King to be a beautiful church. That in no way should it compete [with] Santa Clara.*
>
> *I also heard that when Mexicans would go to ask for assistance there, at Santa Clara, he would send them to the Colonia, saying, "That's the church you should go to." I remember him, "Big Jake." He was big, but it wasn't complimentary. But the church at Santa Clara is so much nicer now.*

Chris Hernandez Perez moved out of the Colonia with her family in the 1950s, but they continued to attend church in the barrio because they felt welcome there.

> *One time I went to Santa Clara. I sat in the pew, and they told me I had to leave. This lady said I shouldn't be sitting in her pew. In those days [the Santa Clara families] had these plaques on the pews. So they moved me and my mom and my sisters, told us to move to the back of the church.… The monsignor was highly prejudiced—Monsignor Jacobs.*
>
> *In fact, just last Sunday I went to Santa Clara. I remember sitting near that pew. Isn't that funny, I remembered right where it was! There are no more plaques, of course. They took out the plaques many years ago, a long time ago.*

It Was Great Candy

Chris Hernandez Perez remembers Father John Fosselman fondly: "Father John, he was the priest at Christ the King that I knew when I was there. I'd go to church and catechism. He always got candy from See's in LA and gave us free candy. It was caramel with marshmallow."

Left: Wedding at Christ the King Church, La Colonia, Oxnard, early 1970s. *Courtesy of Martha Muñoz Rodriguez.*

Below: Exterior of Our Lady of Guadalupe church, La Colonia, Oxnard, 2018. *Photo by author.*

John Martinez liked attending church at Christ the King as well, but for reasons that were a bit more *travieso* (naughty).

> *A lot of us were altar boys. We had a scam! Father John would direct us to give out the candy. We would take turns, and if we were passing it to our friends? They'd get a* bunch *of candy! Then we'd split it later. It was always a lot of candy. It was always in boxes and* quebrada [broken]. *You know, like when they clean out their inventory? It was great candy!*

LAS JAMAICAS

All citizens of La Colonia remember the church as the center of life in the barrio. They worshiped there but also socialized and celebrated at festivals called *jamaicas*. The community would gather to eat, laugh, play games and win prizes, all to benefit the church. Carol Martinez Lopez had an aunt who was a force to be reckoned with when it came to selling food at these events:

> *She had one of those booths, selling tostadas. She had such pride and wanted to make the most money. She took us kids and said, "You're going to help me with my* puesto [booth] *and it's going to be the best. You're going to do it right!" She would show us how. She was an "in charge" type of person.*

Louis Estrada recalls the many *jamaicas* that filled the Colonia calendar:

> *I feel like if there's one thing in my memories that makes me* Mexicano, *it was the* jamaicas. Jamaicas *had a carnival setting; it was fun. There were booths where you could play games and you could win your choice of a duckling or a baby chick.*
>
> *So we would take these baby chicks home and we were so enthralled, so ecstatic about winning and that we had a baby chick. We'd take it home and the adults would put it in the chicken coop. Eventually our grandma would use it for dinner, but we didn't know at the time. Being a child, you'd have these giddy moments of winning something, like a duck. It's so memorable. Well, they were so cute, but now that I look back on it, I see that it was unique, being exposed to that. I've never seen Americans have anything like that.*

Altar of the new Our Lady of Guadalupe during celebration of the Virgin of Guadalupe, La Colonia, Oxnard, 2018. *Photo by author.*

The *jamaicas* were sometimes the backdrop for the juiciest of *chisme* (gossip). Louis's sister Corinne remembers catching a tantalizing glimpse of one such occasion.

> *I went to one of the* jamaicas *with my grandmother; I was about six. I was* metiche [nosy], *always looking at everything and wanting to know what was happening. Next to the church was a little hall. They had like a soda fountain–type area with a counter. My grandpa was sitting at one end of the counter, people were all around, buying menudo, posole, tamales.... Then, suddenly, my grandma grabbed me and yanked me out of the hall! It was too late, though, because I had already seen it.*
>
> *Next to my grandpa there'd been a woman who was feeding him, lovingly spooning little* bocaditos [mouthfuls] *into his mouth. Grandma flew out of there with me, and I was craning my neck to see as much as possible while she was pulling me out of the hall. The weird thing was we remained there at the jamaica; she just took us to the booths outside! When we came home, nothing happened. I never remember them arguing.*

Aurora Lopez leads Colonia girls into the church of Our Lady of Guadalupe for the May processions, La Colonia, Oxnard, 1960s. *Courtesy of Lupe Lujan.*

Corinne also recalls how everyone, no matter their age, participated in the church activities:

> *All the girls dressed in white would be in the front of the church during the month of May to honor the Blessed Mother. We would often wear the dress we made our First Holy Communion in, even if we were* really *outgrowing it! We would wear it until we couldn't anymore. They would have Mass every day, and the girls would line up in their veils....We'd march down the aisle, put down our flower on the altar and then line up back in the pews. In June, it was the boys' turn to honor the Sacred Heart of Jesus, so my brother would have to wear a little suit and the same thing would happen with the boys.*

LAS POSADAS

Louis Estrada particularly loved the more sacred occasions.

> *The* posadas [Mexican processional celebrations] *during Christmas were really something. People would walk down the streets at night, each*

Above: Front yard nativity scene, La Colonia, Oxnard, 2018. *Photo by author.*

Right: Christmas *posada*, La Colonia, Oxnard, 1960s. *Image from* Oxnard Press-Courier.

holding a candle. It was dreamlike to see these flames in the dark. We're talking about hundreds of people, not just ten or twenty; it would fill the darkness like fireflies. I couldn't see where it started or ended, but I could see it because we were on a main street.

FATHER MADERA AND HIS ANGELS

As noted in the *Press-Courier*, the church also had an extraordinary number of activities for teens during the 1960s, thanks to Father Madera's tireless dedication to supporting the Colonia's future leaders.

Madera organized groups such as the aforementioned "Playboys" but also worked with Colonia teens who were in juvenile hall, accompanying them to their court dates. In the *Press-Courier* piece, Father Joe shared how the staff noted his arrival: "Here comes Father Madera after one of his angels."

Some recall the many "firsts" Father Joe brought into their lives: the first time they ever left the Colonia, the first time they ever went ice-skating or played sports. Some even credit Padre Madera with helping them to be the first members of their families to go to college by encouraging them to take advantage of government programs that they would never have known about otherwise. He was also a stable force for those children who had the most unstable lives, dealing with alcoholic parents, perhaps, or siblings who were in gangs.

Father Joe recruited Carol Martinez Lopez and Chris Hernandez Perez, members of his organization for young adults and teens called the Apostleship of the Cross, to be mentors in another group for younger Colonia girls called the Blue Birds. Carol remembers the Blue Birds fondly:

Father wanted us to teach the young girls how to cook, dress and conduct themselves. We were in our early twenties, and we would go to the hall to teach them. When I got engaged, they had a little bridal shower for me. The boys had a service club, too; they would do things for the community.

Rosario Chavez, a longtime friend of Father Joe, recalls his later years:

They had an anniversary [celebration for him] at the Knights of Columbus....It was kind of like a roast. There were at least ten of us [who] were asked to go and speak about Father and what he meant to us.

Interior of the old Our Lady of Guadalupe church, La Colonia, Oxnard, 2018. *Photo by author.*

The girls of the Blue Birds throw a bridal shower for their mentor, Carol Martinez Lopez, *seated with cake*. Standing directly behind her are Chris Hernandez Perez and Father Madera. Martha Muñoz Rodriguez is kneeling in the front row, second from left. The hall was once La Colonia's original place of worship, the Chapel of St. Vianney, Oxnard, 1960s. *Courtesy of Carol Martinez Lopez.*

It was so nice. Each individual felt exactly the same way: that they were special to him. They were made to feel extra special and that he was always there for them. Just like he was for me! It was nice to hear what they had to say, to hear different people's point of view and how they viewed him—so special.

In his later years, Father Joe Madera became Bishop Madera of the Diocese of Fresno, many miles away from Oxnard. There, too, he was known as "the people's bishop" for his affinity with parishioners. He died in 2017.

THE GIFT

Today, the old churches of Cristo Rey and Our Lady of Guadalupe, and even the building that had once been the Chapel of St. Vianney, still stand in La Colonia. But because the number of worshipers with ties to the barrio has increased exponentially since the old days, there is a new large Our Lady of Guadalupe church to accommodate them.

A well-lit open space that gets daily use from the community, the church still offers Masses in both English and Spanish, as well as educational programs. At each day's end, barrio flower vendors bring what's left of their wares to leave as an offering to the statue of the Virgin. Like the old churches, the new *iglesia* does not have fancy stained-glass windows or Gothic arches. But it does have something beautiful and special to look at—something truly unique to La Colonia.

Los Angeles–area artist Lalo Garcia shares his inspiration for this moving mural:

I have had close friends in the city of Oxnard for many years. In fact, there is a huge community of families from my native state of Michoacan, not to mention the village of La Cieneguita, where I was born. My parents have relatives living in Oxnard. As an artist, I have done many exhibits in Oxnard, and as a folklorico *dancer, I performed there many times. So the people there are very familiar to me.*

…I was contacted by Siobhan O'Reilly, the capital campaign manager for the project; she was with Father Roberto Saldivar. I remember him asking me one particular question: "Do you know the meaning of the four-petal flower on Our Lady's tunic? And what it represents?" I shared with him what I knew, and he was very impressed with my explanation.

The Gift, mural by artist Lalo Garcia, La Colonia, Oxnard, 2018. *Photo by author.*

We set up a meeting at the old church, and all he said was that he wanted to see Our Lady depicted in the fields with the workers picking strawberries. That was it.

…We walked into the [site of the new] church. He asked where I thought the mural should go, and I chose the space. Thinking about how he wanted Our Lady in the fields, I thought, "What better way for our parishioners as they leave Mass on Sunday, to look up on their way out and take her with them, to start their week of work?"

I had my share of working on the fields, not strawberries but grapes, which in any case is still field work. But I wanted to refresh my mind; I took a few days and went to the fields and observed the workers and everything else around them, especially what they wear, before I began to sketch anything in my studio. I needed to depict them accurately so that they could identify themselves in that mural.

As for the style, composition and color palette, it is a style that I have been developing [since] 2000. I love the line work, its simplicity on the faceless figures. I wanted to have all the energy coming out of Our Lady's hands, gifting her Son to the workers. The four-petal flower represents Jesus.

When I showed it to Father Roberto, his face was in disbelief. He just said, "I never imagined the mural to look like this, I love it!" We made one modification from my original concept: I had two more angels in the sky; he deleted them….We kept one to represent the [angel] *that's in the original* Tilma [cloak made of cactus fiber on which the original image of Our Lady of Guadalupe was imprinted].

And that was it. I had a month to paint the mural, which I did in a friend of mine's studio in Oxnard.

On dedication day, I remember one lady coming to me. She said, "You painted me! Everybody that works next to me says I'm crazy, because I sing all day long. I tell them, 'I am happy because I have work, and that allows me to feed my children.' And there I am, next to the guy playing the guitar. Thank you!" You can imagine what I felt. And many others could see themselves in those fields as well.

CHAPTER 8

SCHOOL DAYS

THE ELEMENTARY SCHOOLS

Before Ramona and Juanita Schools opened in 1940 and 1951, Colonia children attended school on the other side of the tracks, often in racially segregated classrooms or buildings. Some families chose the option of parochial education at one of Oxnard's Catholic schools, where they felt segregation was not as much of an issue.

Carol Martinez Lopez attended Ramona Elementary School.

> *My mother had an accident when I was a baby and couldn't take care of me. So before I started school, I was raised mainly by an aunt who spoke*

Third graders, Ramona School. La Colonia, Oxnard, 1956. *Courtesy of Lupe Lujan.*

Ramona School, La Colonia, Oxnard, 1950s. *Courtesy of Bungalow Productions.*

Spanish. When I started kindergarten, I remember I was playing jacks with a group of little girls, and the teacher motioned for me to come over to her. She said, "You speak English, no Spanish!"

MENDEZ V. WESTMINSTER

Shortly before the end of World War II, in nearby Orange County, a couple named Gonzalo and Felicitas Mendez enlisted the support of attorney David Marcus and four other families in filing a lawsuit against the segregation of Mexican American children in public schools. The case waged on for two years until finally, with the help of attorney Thurgood Marshall, the court ruled in the Mendezes' favor on April 15, 1947. Two months later, California governor Earl Warren signed a law desegregating schools in the entire state. The landmark *Mendez v. Westminster* case was a key precedent influencing *Brown v. Board of Education* in 1954. For those born in the Colonia after the war, the end of legal segregation meant they would grow up in a very different world than their parents had known.

Ramona School opened seven years before the Mendez case was decided, in 1940, under the pretext of protecting Colonia children from

Felicitas and Gonzalo Mendez, whose landmark case made school segregation illegal in California in 1947. Their daughter, activist Sylvia Mendez, was a central figure in the case. On February 15, 2011, Sylvia was awarded the Presidential Medal of Freedom, the United States' highest civilian honor. *Courtesy of the Mendez family.*

having to cross Oxnard Boulevard to attend elementary schools with non-Hispanic white and Asian children. Juanita School was built in 1951, when the baby boom produced too many children for Ramona to accommodate, even with double sessions cutting the school day in half. Former students remember that both schools were surrounded by barbed-wire fencing, separating them from the surrounding fields.

It wasn't only Mexican American children who attended Ramona and Juanita. The African American families of the Colonia also sent their children to the schools, along with some few non-Hispanic white children. One Colonia native recalls, "There were only occasional Anglos who came to our school; they never stayed long."

WE THOUGHT IT WAS SNOW

In those years following *Mendez v. Westminster*, the fields were an ever-present fixture of a Colonia school day. From the playground, kids could see people hunched over, doing physically grueling and mentally tedious labor. It was a constant reminder that education was their best hope for a better life.

Even after segregation was declared illegal in California, Colonia children were made to take an additional year of school between kindergarten and first grade, called "pre-primary." Oxnard, 1952. *Courtesy of Lupe Lujan.*

Another daily presence were the planes that spread pesticides on the crops during daylight hours, whether there were workers in the fields or not. Ofelia Rodriguez remembers:

> *We would be inside the school when we would hear the planes coming to spray the bean fields. All the kids would run outside. The planes would come and spray. They would come in really low, and we would be out on the playground. The wind would blow, and the pesticides were kind of white. We'd all run to the fence so that the "snow" could fall on us. We would pretend it was snow. Can you believe that? We'd try to catch it on our tongues. I wonder if that's why I got cancer, along with so many kids from my street?*

Ofelia was born and raised on a street that dead-ended onto the lemon orchard. Many families on her block had at least one child during the baby boom who would later develop cancer.

WE ALL GOT ALONG WELL

Those who attended the Colonia elementary schools remember virtually no racial tension during their years there. Many forged lifelong friendships that crossed cultural and racial lines. Fred Rodriguez remembers one such friendship:

In school, we had Latinos, blacks and whites; we all got along well. I had some very good friends from all groups. I remember Hattie Patterson, who was black, she was my friend when we were little. Over the course of the years, we became best friends.

I remember once my mom told me that after I was born, she used to pick lemons along with Hattie Patterson's mom. Mom told me, "When you and Hattie were just born, Mrs. Patterson and I worked in the lemon orchard together. We would take our babies. Whoever was free would nurse them both. If it was me, I'd nurse you and Hattie; if it was Mrs. Patterson, she'd nurse Hattie and you, too." I couldn't wait to tell Hattie the next day at school. She listened, then nodded and said, "Oh yeah, I knew that. That's why we're such good friends!"

Many teachers from the Colonia schools are remembered for their compassion and respect. Fred Rodriguez describes a day he had to stay after school:

I had some very good teachers that I remember fondly. Mrs. Ledesma was my first grade teacher; she was a nice lady. I got to stay with her one day after school because she wanted to talk to me. She spoke to me in Spanish. I couldn't believe it. I thought, "A teacher speaking to me in Spanish?" This was a time when kids could be severely punished and embarrassed for speaking Spanish in school. Speaking Spanish was a reason you would be made to stay after school, so when I stayed after and the teacher spoke to me in Spanish? Wow. She said, "Tienes que ser buen muchacho, no molestas a otros. [You need to be a good boy and not bother the other kids.]" *It really meant a lot to me.*

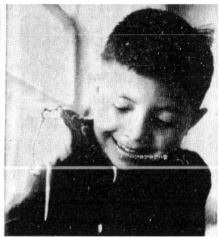

First graders in Juanita School learning science, 1955. *Image from* Oxnard Press-Courier.

THE DOOR PRIZE

Christine Perez Hernandez recalls how difficult school experiences sometimes occurred *outside* the classroom:

> *Looking back, I think in that time there was more prejudice. I wouldn't have thought of it then, that they would be prejudiced toward a Mexican family. For example, my mother would go to our PTA in the evenings. At the meetings, you could win door prizes. They would give certificates for things…to the Americans, though there weren't that many in the Colonia. One time, my mother was so excited because she won the door prize. They gave her a sack of flour. So we carried that big sack of flour all the way back to Garfield Street. My mother said, "Why would I want to win a sack of flour when I hate making tortillas? Bad luck!"*

THE RAMONA SKY ROCKET

Colonia natives often look back on their elementary school days with fondness. In spite of the challenges they faced in the outside world, they say their teachers encouraged them to achieve beyond others' preconceptions. One teacher many credit with making a serious difference was sixth grade

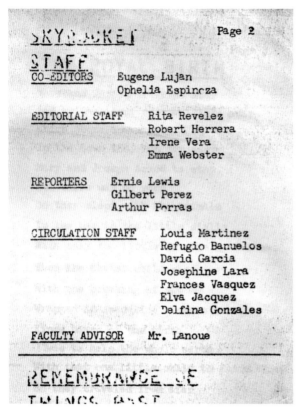

Masthead of *The Ramona Sky Rocket*, produced by Mr. Lanoue's sixth grade class, La Colonia, Oxnard, 1958. *Courtesy of Lupe Lujan.*

teacher Mr. Lanoue. By all accounts, Mr. Lanoue taught the children to believe in themselves and to work together. His 1958 class produced a newspaper, cover to cover, called *The Ramona Sky Rocket*. It's a beautiful example of this teacher's ability to bring out the best in his students and was written collectively by the entire class.

THE CATHOLIC SCHOOLS

According to Colonia kids who attended the Catholic schools, segregation was not a serious issue. Bob Herrera attended both public and parochial schools in Oxnard during the 1940s.

> *I went to Ramona School. Later, I went to Santa Clara. We always liked to go to a Catholic school,* verdad? *My grandma always insisted that we did. Right away, when they brought her from Mexico, she involved herself*

in church. She was a very knowledgeable and sociable person. The house was always full of people visiting.

Santa Clara had the grammar school on the bottom floor, and they built the high school on top. After that, it grew so much that Monsignor Jacobs built the current high school on Saviers Road. Monsignor Jacobs used to be called "Big Jake." The kids, you know how they get things going, they used to make fun of him and stuff like that because he was very strict. But I didn't mind it. He was a very nice person.

Little Brown Marbles, Bouncing Around in a Snowstorm

Corinne Estrada was one of the few Colonia children, along with her brother Louis, who attended Santa Clara Elementary School in the 1960s.

For the most part, we were oblivious [to any prejudice]. *But thinking back…I was the only one getting in trouble.*

I remember there was this nun when I was in the second grade who would get me for anything. For instance, one time I picked up a barrette I found. It was on the floor, and I didn't know who it belonged to. I remember looking at it and admiring it; it was a little butterfly. I guess I wasn't paying attention because [the nun] *came up behind me and said I had stolen it. She held it up and asked who it belonged to, and a blond girl said it was hers. The nun asked, "Did Corinne take this from you?" and the girl said, "Yes." I started to cry, and I said, "No I didn't! No I didn't!" The nun hit my hands for it in front of the class.*

In spite of experiences like this, Corinne wanted to fit in with other kids, who enjoyed rock-and-roll music and something else that was taking Southern California by storm: surfing.

When I was in school, I started to become aware of how it was so cool to be a surfer. All those kids at Santa Clara wanted to be surfers. Nobody in the Colonia knew what that was; I didn't even know how to swim. But because all the cool girls were surfers (they were in eighth grade and I was in fourth), I would say, "I want to be a surfer one day when I grow up…"

I liked a boy named Jerry. He was a little tow head and had a crew cut. He liked the blond girl from the barrette incident. I didn't have blond hair or white skin; I thought Jerry only liked the blondes. That other girl was pretty and always had barrettes and little black velvet bows in her hair, and I had trensas [braids]*! Grandma would always put me in* trensas *and she would curl the ends of the braids and put a bow.*

Lupe Lujan and her sister Aurora De la Selva attended Santa Clara High School on a partial scholarship in the 1960s, while most neighborhood kids attended the public school, Oxnard High. Lupe remembers:

There were only five of us Mexicans from Colonia in our freshman class in the school, and everyone else was white. We were like five little brown marbles, bouncing around in a snowstorm. We felt so strange. All the other girls seemed to know each other on the first day. They were all giggling and asking each other, "Where did you go for vacation?" I had never heard the word "vacation" before! I mean, for us being "on break" from school meant we would be in the fields working with our parents. We'd pick strawberries, which was backbreaking. Or we'd pick lemons, and the huge thorns on the

 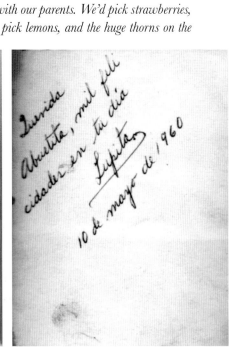

Left: Lupe Lopez school photo, front. La Colonia, Oxnard, 1960. *Courtesy of Lupe Lujan.*

Right: Lupe Lopez school photo, back. "To my dear grandmother, with a thousand best wishes on your special day." La Colonia, Oxnard, 1960. *Courtesy of Lupe Lujan.*

lemon trees would slice you to pieces while you were trying to balance on a ladder. Vacation? What's that?

There was a junior girl on our basketball team who had her own car, a VW bug. I thought, "Wow, she must be rich!" One day she drove us to the North End, the part of Oxnard where the wealthy families lived. They all seemed to be white, too. It was my first time seeing the North End in my life. I couldn't believe my eyes. Some single homes were the size of whole blocks in the Colonia. They had those enormous, circular driveways like you see in the movies. I remember thinking, "Wow, you could fit four of my house in just the driveway!"

MIGHTY YELLOW JACKETS

For Colonia parents whose children were in public school, Oxnard High School was the only option. The old campus was about a thirty-minute walk from the barrio. Manuel Muñoz remembers high school as a very happy time.

I went to Oxnard High and graduated in '58. In the mornings, I would walk to my buddy's house. I had this special whistle so he would know who it was. I'd wait for him, and we'd walk across the street and pick up our other friend. For four years, all three of us would walk to high school; we didn't have a car.

Finally, in our last year, one of us bought a 1949 Ford. Those were the "surfer" days, you know. Kids would go to the beach. One of my buddies wanted to become a barber after graduation, so we drove him all the way to LA just so he could see where the barber school was, so [when the time came] *he could find it on his own.*

Crossing those railroad tracks meant learning for the first time about life outside the Colonia. Some new things were fascinating, like sleepovers or football rallies. Other things—like the abundance of good, nutritious food, brand-new school equipment and state-of-the-art science tools—made Colonia teens slowly realize just how many resources had been denied to them until then. It raised many upsetting questions in a generation that was already asking a lot of questions. Ofelia Rodriguez has memories of leaving the protection she'd felt in the Colonia:

Oxnard High School's 1963 yearbook had a "surfer" theme. *Courtesy of Bungalow Productions.*

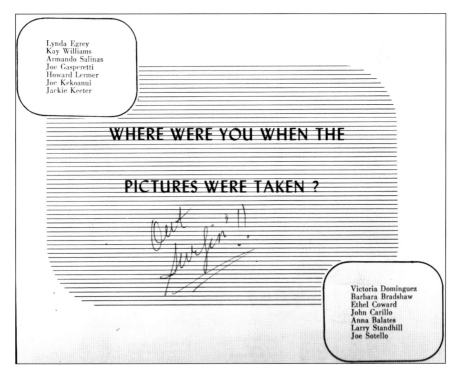

"Camera Shy" list from Oxnard High School yearbook, 1960s. *Courtesy of Bungalow Productions.*

When we crossed the railroad tracks, when we stopped being elementary school children and we actually crossed to the other side, that's when you became aware that you were poor. I still get very emotional about it, yeah, because that's when I became ashamed of being Mexican. That was hard. Before that, you didn't care that you had brown skin. So did everybody else, even the black kids....There was none of this racism that you see today, you know?

Yeah, crossing the tracks was traumatic. You learned about slumber parties and cotillions, and it was like, "Wow, I don't even know what that is." I didn't know anything. People would talk about things that they did, and I didn't know what they were.

For instance, I didn't know what a slumber party was when I was invited to one. I asked my older sister what I should do, and she said maybe take a sleeping bag, so I did. I spent the night, and it was really nice. The next morning, my sister came to pick me up, and we hadn't had

Gymnasium of the old Oxnard High School, 2018. *Photo by author.*

breakfast yet. The hostess asked if I could please stay and have breakfast. My sister had to go to work, and we didn't want to be rude, so I stayed. After breakfast I told them, because I didn't want them to see where I lived, that I would walk home. I walked all the way back to the Colonia alone with my sleeping bag and that was just…it makes me so angry now. It makes me so angry because the [high] school culture was such that it did not comfort us, it did not extend to us the knowledge that, though we might not have had what the other kids had, we were just as rich. Our life was just as rich.

Apart from the emotional challenges of high school for the Colonia kids, Rachel Martinez Sandoval recalls another very practical one: the railroad tracks.

We would take Colonia Road straight out, next to the lemon packinghouse. One memory I have is that, when we went to high school, we'd have to time it so that we could get beyond the tracks before the train came. It would go on and on and on because it was a freight train.

CROSS-COUNTRY

In spite of the difficulties many experienced during those years, Oxnard High also had some very supportive teachers who had a lasting influence in their students' lives. John Martinez remembers one who was particularly impactful.

> *I remember our cross-country coach, Coach Hammond. When he moved here, he wanted to buy a house over there at Carriage Square. And they wouldn't allow him. He was an educated man! That was Bert Hammond.*
>
> *He was a great coach! There we were,* puros Mexicanos y no más él [all Mexicans and just him]. *It was funny because he would scold us when we went to meets in LA—it was big time for us to go to LA! He'd get after us, "You guys better really do this! You'd better follow the rules, you'd better behave. Now, you're going to stand out when you get over there. Don't look at anybody, just do what you gotta do." We would kick a**; we were a bad old team! And then afterwards, he would take us to a restaurant and he goes, "Okay you guys, no stealing of the silverware!"* [laughs]
>
> *Later he taught at Claremont Men's College* [south of Los Angeles]. *After that, when he retired, our old team went down in a van, a bunch of us. His cross-country team. And we surprised him; he had no clue. He seemed really touched.*
>
> *He used to tell us,* era pura verdad [it was pure truth] *if you think about it, he said, "You know, you guys all know each other, you grew up together.* Stick *together. Between all of you, things will happen in your life. You'll go to school, you'll come back, you'll go to the military and do whatever you do…but all of you will have knowledge of something. All of you are going to need each other somewhere along the line."* Y era la verdad. [And it was the truth.] *Now, I'm in my service club. We've got a plumber and guys who do all different kinds of things, and we all help each other out. So he was right with that.* Se ayudan uno al otro. [You help one another.]

Deborah Hammond Kirtman is Bert Hammond's daughter and a graduate of OHS herself. She shares some of her father's insights about his coaching experience at OHS in general and with John's team in particular:

> *When I was in the fourth grade, we moved to Oxnard from upstate New York, where my dad taught at Berkshire Farm.…So when we arrived in*

Left: Bert Hammond had served in World War II and was an officer in the Korean War, 1962. *Courtesy of Bungalow Productions.*

Below: Bert Hammond stands next to the OHS cross-country team, 1962. *Courtesy of Bungalow Productions.*

Oxnard, we knew that many Hispanics were not [considered] "white," and we knew they were not treated as whites. We were not surprised by the presence of Hispanic people. We were surprised by their treatment, which was horrible....Dad was very conversant with the subtleties of race and color when we arrived in Oxnard and even more so after we had lived there for a while.

When Dad became the coach of the Oxnard cross-country team, it was an effort by the head coach to marginalize Dad and his coaching abilities. The head coach was white and from Oklahoma.

Cross-country was not yet an official NCAA sport in Oxnard High School's division. So their meet results were not considered "official," but the team was beating every cross-country team in the state.

All sorts of obstacles were thrown up against this team, consisting mostly of young men whose parents came from Mexico. [There were] *bus drivers who refused to drive unless the team spoke in English and days when* [the team had to arrive at school] *to leave for meets early in the morning but were arrested for loitering at the high school. White people who ran during that time still remember those teams. One runner* [on the Oxnard team] *was nationally ranked. At around that time, Dad was fired over what the head coach described as "a personality conflict."*

Dad knew "what the deal was." He took it to the school board, but they said the head coach had the right to fire him. Dad was also very involved in politics in Oxnard; he was the campaign manager for the first black candidate for either city council or mayor, and he was a member of the Democratic Central Committee. His team saw all of this.

Our entire family was so proud of those runners! Dad wanted them to know that they could accomplish their goals and to not be afraid or ashamed of anything. Many served in the military during the Vietnam War, and at least one of them helped found the Brown Berets. At that time, Oxnard High School did not value their Hispanic students, needless to say. But the disservice ended up only hurting the school.

Team members contacted Dad throughout his life for advice and encouragement. He loved talking with them, and when he retired, Bedford Pinkard [first black elected official in the tri-county area of San Luis Obispo, Santa Barbara and Ventura Counties] *drove a group of former runners to the retirement dinner held at Cal Poly Pomona. Dad was so surprised.*

For Colonia youth, the high school curriculum was largely aimed at preparing students for manual labor. Mexican Americans almost never heard college discussed as a possibility for them. Nevertheless, when they crossed the tracks and faced inequity and bigotry, their talents brought them opportunities they'd never had access to before. Many kids became the first in their families to graduate high school; others became the first to attend college.

But some of the best students in La Colonia weren't kids at all.

Doña Aurora

When Mrs. Aurora Magaña Lopez passed away in 2015 at the age of ninety-two, she was celebrated with one of the biggest and most entertaining memorials in Oxnard history. The throngs of family and friends who attended laughed, sang and even danced in tribute to her extraordinary life and the many people she touched. A common conversation overheard on that day went as follows:

> *"Ah, Doña Aurora! I would never have* [insert fulfilled dream] *if it hadn't been for her! And she always made me feel so special. She always called me 'Mija.'"*
> *"Wait a minute…you weren't 'Mija!' I was 'Mija!'"*

Everyone loved Aurora Lopez, but not everyone knew her story. Her daughter Lupe Lujan shares her mother's remarkable life:

> *You know, you hear from people in the Colonia about how they came to Oxnard to improve their life quality? My mother's took a nosedive when*

Mrs. Aurora Lopez at one of her favorite spots in Oxnard, 1950s. *Courtesy of Lupe Lujan.*

Aurora Magaña, *third row, center*, parades through Guadalajara with her basketball team, 1930s. *Courtesy of Lupe Lujan.*

she came to Oxnard. She'd already been a teacher; in fact, she'd been a principal in Guadalajara.

Back when she was growing up in Guadalajara, Mom was quite the athlete! She played basketball, volleyball and was a tennis star. But she had to stop playing because her brother was killed. Back then, everyone had to stop doing everything and wear black for a whole year, so no more sports for Mom. They couldn't dance, they couldn't go to parties or even the movies.

Despite giving up her favorite activities for a year, Aurora became very accomplished. She played the piano and danced ballet *folklorico*. In 1949, she married Jesus Lopez. Her daughter explains what brought the couple to the barrio:

My parents came to La Colonia because my dad's father lived there. My grandfather was a widower and had remarried to a woman named Josefina. When Dad married my mom and brought her to Oxnard, they lived with my grandfather and Josefina before they got their own place.

I didn't like going to my grandfather's house. He lived on Garfield Street. When we'd arrive, he'd get my dad and take him out to the back porch and offer him a drink from a bottle of wine, something Dad already had a problem with.

With no U.S. teaching credential and limited English fluency, after moving to La Colonia Mom had to stay home raising us kids. But then

Aurora Lopez going to her job at Camarillo State Hospital, 1970s. *Courtesy of Lupe Lujan.*

my dad stopped working, so Mom had to work—at the packinghouse, the chilería, Stokely's and, of course, the fields.

The first time she had an opportunity to get out of the fields was when Mr. Anguiano, Joe Anguiano, got her an opportunity at 3M Company. Working there, she eventually qualified for a War on Poverty program initiated by President Johnson. With that program, she enrolled in the nursing course at Ventura College. She completed her first year, but there were no spots for the second year. So she decided to become a psychiatric technician because the classes she had already done were transferrable. She graduated with her technician state license and got a job at Camarillo State Hospital.

My mom did such a good job at Camarillo State Hospital that they offered her a scholarship to go to college at Cal Lutheran. This meant she could work toward her U.S. teaching credential. So she would go to classes and still work at the hospital.

After years of raising children and dealing with the very limited opportunities available to women in the Colonia, Aurora Lopez went back to college at forty-nine. She eventually earned her BS, master's degree in special education and teaching credential. She continued to work at the hospital, where she was joined by her son Jesus.

She worked with different groups in different units, like the autistic children and developmentally delayed adults. My brother was also working there

Aurora Lopez on graduation day
about to receive her master's degree,
1970s. *Courtesy of Lupe Lujan.*

*as a psych tech, and he would be her assistant. Back then, they would use
a lot of ECT [electroconvulsive therapy], but my mom and brother,
they wouldn't use it. Mom would play the piano for the patients and my
brother would sing; they used music as a reward to modify the patient's
behavior. The hospital used to do these audits where they would bring the
VIPs around. My mom got a commendation for the way they observed her
and my brother handling the class. They requested my mom to be there when
they did the exit interviews because they wanted to recognize her. She worked
really, really hard.*

Camarillo State Hospital closed in the 1990s; it's now the site of Cal State
Channel Islands. When her time there had ended, Aurora embarked on yet
another career where she would influence even more lives: she went back to
teaching. It wasn't her plan; she was simply helping her daughter Lupe, who
was a teacher in Oxnard. Lupe's husband, Gene, also a Colonia native, was
fighting terminal cancer. He was in his forties.

*When my husband got cancer, I would teach for half the day and go to LA
to be with him in the hospital. My younger sister moved in to help take care
of my son, who was very young, because I wouldn't get back from LA until*

143

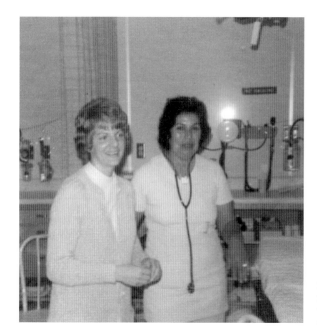

Aurora Lopez, *right*, at her job at Camarillo State Hospital, 1970s. *Courtesy of Lupe Lujan.*

after 10:00 p.m. When I knew Gene wasn't leaving the hospital, I begged my mom to take my class for me because there were hardly any bilingual teachers, so she took over my class for three months. She was so well liked that, after that, all my teacher friends would always request my mom to sub for them! So she ended up doing a lot of substitute teaching for the Oxnard school district.

In addition, Aurora began to teach English as a Second Language to parents at Cesar Chavez and Ramona School, again assisted by her son Jesus. She was also enlisted by family members Clara Ramos and Imelda Almanza to participate in California's early education program, First Five, and the Oxnard District's Migrant Program. Aurora taught parents the English, writing and reading skills they'd need to increase the opportunities they had available to them.

But she didn't stop there.

Mom also collaborated with Ventura College in presenting workshops on domestic violence. Mom did that for years, but she stopped when my brother Chuy got sick.

After my brother died, she didn't want to do the same kind of work she'd done with him. So she began to work with the Mexican consulate. She

144

Aurora Lopez at one of many workshops she conducted at Ventura College, 2000s. *Courtesy of Lupe Lujan.*

was teaching reading in Spanish to different ethnic groups. She worked on everything!

After Mom died, the consulate dedicated a room to her. They called it "Salon Aurorita," and it has a huge portrait of her. They did this unveiling where they invited all of us, along with representatives from the city and many other organizations.

My mom loved to be with people, and she always made everybody feel special. She would be so excited about whatever they were interested in. So the "Salon Aurorita" is used for community functions: classes, presentations, workshops, cultural festivities.

When Aurora's family decided to set up a scholarship in her name, the consulate agreed to contribute to her lasting legacy. The Aurora Lopez Scholarship, available through the Ventura College Foundation, is designated for women who want to be teachers.

Sometimes I ask myself, "Would Mom have done all of those things, accomplished all she did, if things had been better with my dad?" She used to lament that her accent was so thick, but it never stopped her. So, if she had had the opportunities she worked so hard to give to younger people, I wonder what she would have done with them. She knew that if you have a good solid education, it makes things a lot easier.

CHIQUES

D on W. Martin concluded his five-part series on La Colonia for the *Oxnard Press-Courier* on July 24, 1963.

> *By the time you have spent many days and evenings in Colonia, and chatted with dozens of residents, many of your questions have been answered.*
>
> *Some of these answers surprise you.*
>
> *…But the real answers to Colonia's problem lies in two areas, one intertwined with the other. These are youth and understanding….New understanding, spurred by fresh, new ideas and the vigor of youth, must continue if Colonia is to win its battle for dignity.*

Today, the lemon orchard is an upscale housing development, and a "pachuco" is someone exploring their culture through vintage fashion. There are at least a dozen high schools in Greater Oxnard.

In La Colonia, life continues in many ways as it always has, only with many more cars around. Among the sounds of neighbors chatting with one another over the traffic, you might catch a term only the real locals use: *Chiques*.

Some say that, at first, it was a word used by those from La Colonia to refer to the city of Oxnard. Manuel Muñoz shares some final memories and an early legend of this mysterious word's origin.

> *In the late '40s, when we got back on our feet after the war, I used to go to see the Estrada brothers. I got to enjoy the music of their band.…Let me tell you, it was marvelous. They were the best years of my life, actually.*

From left to right: Mauro Muñoz, Albert Muñoz, "Butch" Muñoz, family friend, John Muñoz and Manuel Muñoz. *Courtesy of Martha Munoz Rodriguez.*

In the '50s? Every day for four years we crossed the tracks, we walked to the high school and back. It was nice. Heck yeah, you'd stop by Peacock's Record Bar and have a banana split or a root beer float…like Happy Days. *You know, with the Fonz and all that stuff? Same atmosphere.*

Not 'til our kids came home from the Vietnam War did everything start to build up. Before that, there was happiness and there was tragedy. I never had any enemies at all; what for? We all joined together, "comrades in arms," like they say.

You know what our neighborhood called Oxnard back in those days? It was a nickname: Chiques. *I was wondering about that once, so I asked my uncle, "How come we got the name of* Chiques*?" You know why? Because of the movies. They would pass through town, on their way up the coast to Santa Barbara or Port Hueneme Harbor or someplace fancy like that, to film a scene. But they used to stop in Oxnard. In those days, everybody had chickens, and the kids would bring them around the tourists. The film people would say, "Oh, look at those chickies!" You know, little* pollitos*?* Chickies. *Those kids grew up, and the rest of our lives the name of Oxnard was* Chiques. *That's what my uncle said. "Well, there were a lot of tourists around here, and they called the kids 'chicks.'* Chickies. Chiques*."*

BIBLIOGRAPHY

Interviews

Joe Anguiano. Interviewed August 12, 2018.
Rachel Anguiano. Interviewed August 12, 2018.
Eddie Cabral Jr. Interviewed August 11, 2018.
Ofelia Cabral. Interviewed August 11, 2018.
Richie Cabral. Interviewed August 11, 2018.
Dr. Richard Griswold del Castillo. Interviewed December 14, 2018.
Rosario Chavez. Interviewed August 11, 2018.
Ruben Espinoza. Interviewed October 7, 2018.
Corinne Estrada. Interviewed May 6, 2018.
Louis Estrada. Interviewed May 6, 2018.
Dr. Elvia Estrella. Interviewed December 3, 2018.
Lalo Garcia. Interviewed May 29, 2018.
Robert Herrera. Interviewed August 11, 2018.
Eric Humel. Interviewed August 8, 2018.
Deborah Hammond Kirtman. Interviewed January 3, 2019.
Carol Martinez Lopez. Interviewed November 17, 2018.
Lupe Lopez Lujan. Interviewed April 27, 2018, and September 22, 2018.
John Martinez. Interviewed November 17, 2018.
Manuel Muñoz. Interviewed September 26, 2018, and September 27, 2018.
Christine Hernandez Perez. Interviewed November 17, 2018.
Fred Rodriguez. Interviewed April 27, 2018.

Martha Muñoz Rodriguez. Interviewed June 25, 2018, and September 23, 2018.

Ofelia Espinoza Rodriguez. Interviewed April 27, 2018.

Rachel Martinez Sandoval. Interviewed November 17, 2018.

Aurora Lopez de la Selva. Interviewed April 27, 2018.

Bruce Smith. Interviewed August 11, 2018.

Catalina Frazier Soria. Interviewed December 16, 2018.

Isabel Soria. Interviewed December 16, 2018.

Secondary Sources

Barajas, Frank P. *Curious Unions: Mexican American Workers and Resistance in Oxnard, California, 1898–1961*. Lincoln: University of Nebraska Press, 2012.

Bird, Mike. "Beloved 'Roberto' Honored in Colonia in Life, Death." *Oxnard Press-Courier*, June 6, 1968, 19.

Bitters, Bill. "Failed to Read English—Four Barred from Voting." *Oxnard Press-Courier*, November 9, 1960, 19.

Brown, Charles A., et al. "Johnson Theory Disputed." *Oxnard Press-Courier*, May 6, 1969, 7.

Castillo, Richard Griswold del. *Chicano San Diego: Cultural Space and the Struggle for Justice*. Tucson: University of Arizona Press, 2007.

Congressional Medal of Honor Society. "Rascon, Alfred V." www.cmohs.org/recipient-detail/3397/rascon-alfred-v.php.

De Backer, Cathy. "Ball Funds Earmarked for Expanded Legal Aid." *Oxnard Press-Courier*, January 20, 1966, 10.

Denman, Bob. "Kennedy's County Visit: Campaign Memories." *Oxnard Press-Courier*, June 6, 1968, 19.

———. "Political Hoopla in County Thousands Greet RFK." *Oxnard Press-Courier*, May 29, 1968, 1.

Douglas, John. "Jewell Promises Force to Quell Colonia Gangs: Chief Paints Grim Picture of Area." *Oxnard Press-Courier*, March 2, 1967, 1.

García, David G. *Strategies of Segregation: Race, Residence, and the Struggle for Educational Equality*. Berkeley: University of California Press, 2018.

Grimes, George. "This Is Oxnard." *Oxnard Press-Courier*, October 15, 1952, 1.

Hartmann, Bea. "Brown Berets Aggressive in Spirit, Energetic." *Oxnard Press-Courier*, August 22, 1968, 17.

———. "Colonia Statement 'Ridiculous'—Jewell." *Oxnard Press-Courier*, August 10, 1968, 1.

———. "Who Are the Guys in Brown Berets?" *Oxnard Press-Courier*, August 21, 1968, 15.

Johnson, Henry J. "Voice of the People: Busing Pupils Would Result in 'Cultural Contamination.'" *Oxnard Press-Courier*, April 30, 1969, 7.

Levy, Jacques E., and Cesar Chavez. *Cesar Chavez: Autobiography of La Causa*. Minneapolis: University of Minnesota Press, 2007.

MacKay, Ned. "Colonia Group Hits School Integration Plan." *Oxnard Press-Courier*, June 17, 1970, 1.

Mandel, Stan. "Creatures of Every Description 'Enrolled' in Classes." *Oxnard Press-Courier*, February 23, 1955, 8.

Martin, Don W. "A Catholic Priest's Investment in Colonia's Youth." *Oxnard Press-Courier*, July 23, 1963, 5.

———. "Colonia's Answers: They Will Come, but Slowly." *Oxnard Press-Courier*, July 24, 1963, 8.

———. "Colonia's Hard Battle for Dignity." *Oxnard Press-Courier*, July 19, 1963, 1.

———. "Colonia Workers Rise and Retire with the Sun." *Oxnard Press-Courier*, July 22, 1963, 9.

———. "Equality for Domestics: The Sorry Plight of Local Workers." *Oxnard Press-Courier*, June 14, 1963, 3.

———. "Henry Thomas Oxnard Built a Factory, and Created a Town from a Barley Field." *Oxnard Press-Courier, PC The Weekly Magazine*, August 21, 1966, 6.

———. "Long-time Colonia Resident Is Bitter." *Oxnard Press-Courier*, July 20, 1963, 4.

McCormick, John. "Oxnard Police Quell Fights; Girl Struck by Stray Bullet." *Oxnard Press-Courier*, September 19, 1966, 1.

Mount, Robert. "Coastal Valley Canning Vital Cog in Local Economy." *Oxnard Press-Courier*, October 5, 1962, 6.

Nielsen, Rick. "Police Quell Disturbance in Colonia." *Oxnard Press-Courier*, March 17, 1975, 1.

Orthuber, Gerhard, et al. "Voice of the People: School Desegregation 'Contamination Theory' Hit." *Oxnard Press-Courier*, May 6, 1969, 7.

Oxnard Press-Courier. "An Authentic Mexican Posada." December 23, 1970, 14.

———. "Bank Gutted in UCSB Rampage." February 26, 1970, 1.

———. "Chavez on Politics, Labor." April 3, 1968, 13.

———. "Chavez Predicts Growers' Defeat." October 23, 1970, 6.

———. "Child Scalded to Death in Fall into Boiling Water." October 17, 1941, 1.

———. "Christ the King Church to Build New Grade School." December 31, 1954, 9.

———. "City Council Candidate John Soria Favors Oxnard-Hueneme Consolidation." March 25, 1960, 3.

———. "Colonia Folk Send Flowers to Arlington." June 9, 1968, 2.

———. "Colonia March Mourns RFK." June 10, 1968, 22.

———. "Council Learns New Methods to Draw Votes." August 12, 1959, 3.

———. "CSO Opens Drive to Get Out Vote." November 1, 1958, 8.

———. "Due in Colonia: Kennedy Tours Oxnard Tuesday." May 27, 1968, 13.

———. "Editorial: Carrot and Stick." March 16, 1967, 8.

———. "Editorial: The Poverty Pickets." May 28, 1965, 10.

———. "Editorial: Who Are the Brown Berets?" August 20, 1968, 8.

———. "Esther Navarro, Robert Herrera Wed in Oxnard." July 1, 1957, 5.

———. "Father John Fosselman Is Honored." October 27, 1955, 3.

———. "Friends Offer to Take Soria Children; Oldest Boy Strives to Keep Family United." September 6, 1945, 1.

———. "Industry Leaders Briefed on MAOF." February 1, 1968, 17.

———. "Last Class on Double Sessions Ends." November 12, 1954, 1.

———. "Louis Soria, 16, Hopes to Keep Family United." September 5, 1945, 1.

———. "Mexican American of the Year Named." December 12, 1967, 27.

———. "Mob Attacks Local Police; Officers Called to Quell Mexican Riot on Boulevard." October 28, 1940, 1.

———. "NAACP Marches for Desegregation." December 3, 1969, 1.

———. "101 Liquor Store Held Up Again." September 15, 1960, 1.

———. "Oxnard Trustees OK More Study for Racial Balance Plan." November 5, 1969, 25.

———. "Oxnard Veteran Gets Silver Star." August 1, 1966, 1.

———. "Police Quell Fights; Looked Bad at First." December 18, 1961, 1.

———. "Police Quell Pachuco Riot." October 4, 1944, 1.

———. "Prejudice Discussion Scheduled April 21 at Juanita School." April 12, 1958, 3.

———. "Racial Discrimination Denied at Meeting." April 22, 1958, 3.

———. "Snowfall Makes History." January 11, 1949, 1.

———. "Soria Children May Get Home." September 7, 1945, 1.

———. "Start Christmas Early by Going the Posada Route." November 26, 1964, 15.

———. "Students Reveal Strong Views on Recreation Center." April 4, 1958, 10.

———. "Sugar Factory Is Best Known Industry in Oxnard District." August 30, 1941, 12.

———. "Useful Help." October 30, 1952, 20.

Sherry, Kevin F. "This Woman's Place Is in the Ring." *Los Angeles Times*, May 7, 2001. articles.latimes.com/2001/may/07/local/me-60398.

Sopkin, Elliott. "Bert Hammond Charges Racial Discrimination: Can't Buy North Oxnard Home, Teacher Claims." *Oxnard Press-Courier*, August 22, 1962, 36.

Tatten, Hal. "Time Out!" *Oxnard Press-Courier*, April 13, 1950, 7.

———. "Time Out!" *Oxnard Press-Courier*, October 22, 1952, 5.

Werkman, Dirk. "UFW's Chavez Pledges to Put Strikers in Jails." *Oxnard Press-Courier*, June 2, 1974, 1.

White, Dave. "Barbershop Brothers Make the Music Scene." *Oxnard Press-Courier, PC The Weekly Magazine*, January 29, 1967, 5.

Zavala, Laura. "Voice of the People: Wishes Ignored?" *Oxnard Press-Courier*, June 9, 1970, 7.

RECOMMENDED READING
FOR ALL AGES

Casilla, Robert, and Sarah Warren. *Dolores Huerta: A Hero to Migrant Workers*. N.p.: Two Lions, 2012.

Gonzalez, Martín Alberto. *21 Miles of Scenic Beauty…and Then Oxnard: Counterstories and Testimonies*. N.p.: Martín Alberto Gonzalez, 2017.

Krull, Kathleen, and Yuyi Morales. *Harvesting Hope: The Story of Cesar Chavez*. Columbus, OH: Zaner-Bloser, 2013.

Marin, Cheech. *Cheech Is Not My Real Name: but Don't Call Me Chong!* New York: Grand Central Publishing, 2018.

Moraga, Cherríe. *Native Country of the Heart*. New York: Farrar, Straus & Giroux, 2019.

Serros, Michele M. *Chicana Falsa*. N.p.: Lalo Press, 1994.

Tonatiuh, Duncan. *Separate Is Never Equal: The Story of Sylvia Mendez and Her Family's Fight for Desegregation*. New York: Abrams Books for Young Readers, 2014.

ABOUT THE AUTHORS

Sandra and Margo Porras, Oxnard, 1974.
Courtesy Bungalow Productions.

Margo Porras is a writer and designer. She's contributed to numerous media outlets, including *San Diego Magazine*, *Mamiverse* and *SheKnows* (Digiday Publishing Award). Margo and her work have been featured in many print publications, including *Women's Day*, *Latina* and the *New York Times*. She's also the longtime co-host of the culture podcast *Book vs. Movie*. Margo and her husband, Todd, live in her native San Diego, where she enjoys working at KPBS, reading to her kids and writing about herself in the third person. This is her first book.

Sandra Porras is a retired educator and education activist who has been writing all her life. A native Oxnardian, she has previously been featured in *Pronto, Roma*. She lives in San Diego and is a proud grandmother to her three grandchildren.